More Words of Wisdom

for Everyday Living

Also by Andrew and Helen W A Hain:

Living the Spiritual Laws
for Health and Abundance

Words of Wisdom
for Everyday Living

More Words of Wisdom

for Everyday Living

Andrew Hain
Helen W A Hain

Well Within Therapies
26 Orchard Road
Kingston upon Thames
KT1 2QW
Telephone 020 8549 1784

Disclaimer
Every care is taken to ensure that the routines, methods and processes that are
set out herein are suitable to individuals of all levels of fitness. However,
please note that such material may not be suitable for all. If you have any
doubts, seek medical advice prior to commencement. Cease the program
immediately should you experience any discomfort and seek medical advice.

Cover Illustration: The Beginning by Andrew Hain Copyright © 2003

ISBN 9780954544621

Printed and bound by CPI Antony Rowe, Eastbourne

Contents

29. Operate from the heart but remember the fuel it needs is love.
30. Nourish your mind as well as your body.
31. When one door shuts look for one that is open.
32. You cannot buy peace but you can create it.
33. The best healer you need is yourself
34. Self judgment brings forth purer intentions
35. Conserve energy -- don't waste it in negative directions
36. Do your best then ask the Universe to do the rest
37. Learn from the past but don't keep reliving it
38. Listen to others' points of view but remember you don't have to accept them as your own
39. Never waste time – you cannot reclaim it
40. See with your Soul and notice how better the view is
41. Spring clean your mind to clear away the debris
42. The lighter your load, the faster you travel
43. If you shine like the stars you will be seen in the darkness
44. If you think you're a failure you've failed to think positively
45. Tell the Universe your difficulties but let it decide how to deal with them
46. You are the driver on your pathway. Don't blame others if you don't reach your destination.
47. There is much to learn from nature but you need to take time to connect
48. Not everyone can see Angels but everyone can ask them for help
49. It's not just friends who are special, enemies are too
50. Don't give up, link up

Epilogue   Spiritual Progression

Preface

This book is a follow-up to "Words of Wisdom for Everyday Living" and is a result of what we have received for our own guidance and evolution.

Once again, we have shared what we have been given hoping it provides insight and upliftment to others. It is no substitute for your own intuition and we urge you to follow your own inner light. No one path is right for everyone but sharing what we each receive can benefit many. There is no fast track to spiritual evolution and most of us need support at some stage of our journey. We appreciate the support and guidance we have received on our journey, and believe that giving and receiving are vital for us all to attain enlightenment.

Whilst this book can be read from cover to cover, we hope that, when you require upliftment and inspiration, you will take a few moments quiet to ask for guidance and then open the book at random and see what you are given.

We have also posed questions at the end of each motto to assist you in seeking your own answers. It's your Inner Guidance that is important as truth for you is what resonates within you.

We have found that the only way for us when faced with difficult situations was to go within and seek guidance at a spiritual level. All we seek to do with our writings, not only in this book, but also in "Living the Spiritual Laws for Health and Abundance" and "Words of Wisdom for Everyday Living", is to share what we found helpful and to encourage the reader to find their own spiritual answers.

This takes determination, and ensuring that time is regularly allocated for quiet times is vital. This is taking care of yourself, loving yourself, and others will automatically benefit too.

Keeping a journal of your experiences each day and noting the assistance received from the Higher Realms has been for us a source of support and upliftment. We hope that you, too, will find the same benefit from the words in this book and from the truth that resides within you.

In this book we will, at times, exhort you to join with nature. Indeed we have done this in our past books. Most of what you will read in this book has been channelled whilst we have done just that. We have gone to what we find are pleasant, tranquil locations. We have sat there admiring the scenery and listening to the sounds. Then we have gone into the quiet and channelled the words that form this book (as we have done for past writings, too).

AH & HWAH

1. Keep an open mind or you may shut out the truth

You have found it hard to shake off beliefs bestowed on you by well meaning people who thought it their duty to do so. This is the way they give love. It is full of demands that you accept what is right for them. You have been expected to take on these beliefs unconditionally, and without question. This you did, particularly as a child and adolescent. Your parents' beliefs became your beliefs. In fact they were beliefs given to them by their parents and were never questioned. You weren't expected to question them either. You took on these beliefs with the fear that, if you questioned them or discarded them, something awful could happen.

As you read and developed, you accessed others' beliefs which were different to those you'd been taught. Your mind opened. You meditated on this, and allowed yourself to gradually accept what felt right for you. You realised the importance of keeping an open mind, knowing that what is right and true for you at one moment may alter as time goes by. You are now allowing yourself to be yourself and to discriminate information bombarding you. Take time each day to be still, to empty the mind of preconceived ideas. Ask yourself, "What is right for me now?" and take this on board. Does it feel right? Can you hold this as truth? You cannot progress and develop if you have a closed mind. No new thoughts can enter, and stagnation takes place.

There are times when you come across new ideas and you begin to pay more attention to whose they are rather than to what they say. Do not judge ideas in this way. Is the idea something you accept or not? Read widely, meditate on the wisdom and hold on to what seems true. But never hold on tight, just remember them and when the time is right to move on in your thinking, release them to make room for new ideas and knowledge. As you read, separate ideas from the author. You do not have to accept everything that that person says. Dip in to many places, taking what feels right and leaving behind what doesn't. Do not judge: just take what you feel is true, and give thanks for the wisdom whilst remembering that you may be letting go of these ideas at a future date.

As you meditate and get in touch with your Higher Self you will grow spiritually, and the knowledge you have today may no longer serve any purpose in the future. This is why you must never force your ideas on others. Why should they accept what you may reject in the future? By all means share your ideas and knowledge with others, as they will serve some, but never force these onto others. Allow them freedom. Allow them the opportunity of having an open mind and the truth that is right for them will come at the right time.

The mind is a wonderful thing. Everything that is your reality is created here. Everything you believe in is located here. Every time you make a judgment you do so because of what is in your mind. If it is in your mind, it is in your body. If it is a closed environment then nothing gets in and all your biases get out. It is one way traffic. Have you ever looked beyond what you think? Have you considered alternatives? What do you think of other people's views? There is nothing easier than making snap judgments based on little evidence and the experience of your closed mind. Do you ever think that there could be something missing? The facts maybe? The truth? Mitigating evidence? Nothing is ever black and white. Always there are shades of grey.

Open up your mind and a whole world of possibilities springs alive. Don't believe everything you hear or read. Look behind the façade to see what else lies there. Have you ever wondered what was behind the high wall that surrounds a closed mind? Maybe a jungle full of danger, maybe a garden so beautiful you could wander round it forever.

Take a look over the wall. Who knows what you will see. Better still knock the wall down and become at one with the world. It takes great courage to do this but help is always at hand. Don't ever think you are alone, as this is never the case. Your Inner Self can connect you to the help you need, and is always connected to that line of communication. You don't use it often enough. Maybe it was outside your wall and you didn't know it was there. Explore your mind: you will find that there are no boundaries and the wall is of your own making. You may have heard it said "the truth is out there" so go find it.

You cannot progress and develop if you have a closed mind.

Do you have fixed ideas about subjects such as money, love, sharing?
Take time to consider your views and ask yourself if they are holding you back spirituality in any way.

How willing are you to listen to others' ideas? Sharing of ideas and knowledge opens us up to new ways of thinking, but remember to take on board only what you feel to be right for you.

2. Change brings growth and growth brings new potential

So many of you have blinkers and ear muffs as if you are afraid something new will disturb you. Truth comes in stages. You would not be able to understand or take in everything at once. You would not explain everything you knew to a young child. He would switch off and learn nothing. You break down what you wish him to learn into simple language and give him a bit at a time. This allows him to grow and learn at his own pace. You only tell him something when you think he is ready to receive it.

A child is given facts by his parents and teachers, and, with the best of intentions this knowledge contains their beliefs and ideas. A young child rarely questions what he is told and accepts the information which he stores in his mind. As adults we need to reassess our learnings, retaining what feels right and rejecting what no longer serves us. Reject with love and be grateful for what was given, as it was right at that time and served a useful purpose.

The stages you have gone through have led you along your path. Be open and willing to receive new ideas and knowledge but be willing to change these and accept new ones as you grow spiritually. By clinging on to rigid ideas and refusing to change you cannot grow. Growth comes from change and the path of enlightenment has many stages which require completion. Flowers don't grow and blossom overnight. You can't even see the changes happening they are so subtle. The beauty unfolds at the right time. Go with what feels right, remembering not to condemn others for their beliefs, but understanding that their beliefs are right for them at their own stage of progress. An open mind enables you to reach your full potential, to love yourself and allows you to give love to others and accept them as they are.

When you go about your life in the same way as you have always done, you are only ploughing one furrow so to speak. Up and down the same track time after time. All you are doing really is digging a rut for yourself. The walls will get taller the more you dig. Don't you ever think there is another way? What lies beyond the walls of your rut? Is life tedious ploughing this long lonely furrow?

What you need to do is to stop digging and consider what it is you are doing. What does it achieve? Is that what you want? If it is then continue doing as you do.

However, if it is not then you need to change something. Maybe you need to change everything. Who knows, but you? In that moment of changing your routine, you grow. You develop. You are breaking new ground. Your whole being grows. As you learn new ways, techniques, facts, your spiritual bodies expand. Your personal experience enlarges, enriches, giving you new confidence, new ambition, new hope. Change has done this for you. It is what change is all about. Having changed once you can change again because your first change needn't be your only one. Having reaped the benefits or gained the experience, you now have the potential to keep evolving, to continue growing.

It is a cycle: change brings growth, growth brings experience, experience brings hope, and hope brings potential. It goes on and on. It is more spiral than circular because as the spiral develops it grows upwards and outwards.

This is not to say that you should always be changing. There will be times when you need to stop to let it all sink in. However, it is helpful to always keep an open mind and be prepared to change. After all, if water, the basis of life, doesn't move it becomes stagnant. Don't stay in the rut too long.

An open mind enables you to reach your full potential.

What small changes could you make immediately to assist your growth, eg daily walk in nature, reading inspirational writing or learning a new skill?

If we don't change we just remain static. Do you fear new possibilities or are you willing to change in order to reach your full potential?

3. Problems come to teach us something: if you don't learn you'll drown in the experience

If everything in life was pleasant and simple we would gain nothing and progress would be hindered. Problems and situations come to us for a reason. When faced with a difficult situation it is easy to be immersed in it, and be overwhelmed by emotions. It can be difficult to take your attention away to other things. We become ill as there seems to be no way out. If we don't learn from the experience a new one will confront us to give us another opportunity to grow. It is easy to go into a downward spiral and feel as if the world is against us.

With each problem ask what brought it to you, and what you can learn from it. Does it teach you to acquire new skills, change your attitude or way of life? View it as an opportunity for spiritual growth and thank it for presenting itself. Fighting it will cause you to get caught up in a spiral of negativity, and the deeper you go, the harder it is to fight your way back. Take time to sit quiet, step back from the problem and view it from a distance. Ask for the reason it is there and be prepared to act positively so that you can move on. Each problem surmounted will add to your coping skills, and, no matter what you are faced with, you will stay afloat, so drowning will be a thing of the past.

There is nothing that happens just for its own sake. Always there is a reason for an incident, an event, an occurrence, call it what you will. Chance encounters? They don't exist either. Always, there is a reason.

So when problems come along they haven't done so just to spite you or cause you frustration and anger. They have come to show you something, to reveal some aspect or piece of insight. Really, they have come to teach you something.

If you are having the problem then the message or lesson is for you. It may also involve others, but others will have to work out what their message is. You need to be looking for the message directed at you.

It will be something personal. For instance, it may be about your relationships with others, it may be about how you perceive your own self worth, it may be a lesson in trusting the Universe. It could be anything and it is beneficial to look for what it is.

When you do decipher the message and understand the lesson, you can move on physically, emotionally, mentally or spiritually or on any combination of these levels.

Sometimes we may miss the message, or even fail to look for it. There may be good and valid reasons for this: indeed, this might even be a lesson in itself. However, the message will be retransmitted until we decipher it.

Herein lies the need for us to look at the details of our lives. We need to be aware that the Universe is sending us messages in very subtle ways, and it will continue to send out the same message until we understand.

However, if we fail completely to look for the message, or deny that one exists, we are in great danger of accumulating incidents, events, occurrences or problems in our life. Life will become one huge problem. We will stumble from crisis to crisis. Perhaps the question will be asked, "Why me?" but is it ever answered?

The "why me" is the Universe giving you the biggest hint it can that you have a message waiting to be discovered. You risk being overwhelmed by events if you do not attempt to seek out the message the Universe is trying to convey to you. Until you look you won't discover, and until you discover you will continue to be inundated.

Is there a message for you here and now?

> **With each problem ask what brought it to you, and what you can learn from it.**
>
> Are you experiencing a current difficulty? If so, what can you learn from it eg be more forgiving, etc.?
>
> Can you identify a problem you were faced with in the past which later in life gave you the courage or skills to cope with a difficulty that arose?

4. Too much reasoning swallows up the truth

Truth is what feels right to your innermost being. Become silent, allowing your conscious, analytical mind to rest and you will know intuitively what is right for you now. As you grow and develop be prepared for your ideas to change. What is right for you now will alter as you open up more on your spiritual pathway.

Your conscious mind will bombard you with knowledge and ideas you have absorbed from others, and will try to convince you that you should hold these beliefs for ever. Truth becomes lost if you look for scientific proof. Many forms of healing bring results although the way in which they work cannot be proved. Many people miss out on the benefits as they want to understand the reasoning behind them before being willing to experience the results. Open up to your feelings, trust them, and give truth a chance.

When confronted by any situation or dilemma it is best if you can take time to ascertain the facts. To make snap, instantaneous judgments or decisions can have far reaching consequences, especially if you turn out to have made a poor or wrong decision.

It is more helpful to find out what the truth of the matter is and thus we need to strive as much as we can to carry out as full an inquiry as possible in the circumstances. When all of the facts are in front of us an honest decision can then be made.

However it is best if we do not take too long to do this, for the temptation will be to go over and over the matters until we confuse ourselves. By dwelling on items we allow indecision to creep in, and indecision will cause us to feel uncertain.

We will overcomplicate the situation by asking more and more questions. Self doubt will prevail and instead of coming to a reasoned, lucid outcome, we will have drowned in a morass of uncertainty. Far from having a certain outcome we will have one filled by doubt and misgiving. We will have no confidence in our answer.

Establish the facts, make contact with your Inner Self, ask the Universe for help, then decide. You will find that with Source and your Inner Being behind you, your decision making will be accurate and you can act in total confidence.

> **Open up to your feelings, trust them, and give truth a chance.**

To what extent are you willing to try out new ideas? Could you benefit from experiencing something you have dismissed up until now?

What do you trust most – your critical conscious mind or your inner feelings?

5. Trust dispels fear but fear attracts more fear

Trust is a quality which will carry you peacefully through any situation in life. It is the ability to be in the present, acknowledging its value and the lessons it holds, without worrying about future outcomes. It's the ability to face up to challenges, whatever they may be, head on, knowing that you will be taken care of. Everything happens for a reason which is not always apparent, but by trusting that it is all part of God's plan, you will find the strength to cope and you will learn from it.

Love whatever confronts you. Trust that it is right for your growth and there will be no place for fear.

Fear is loss of trust in God and the Universe. If you are afraid, it is impossible to face up to events with love and learn from them. The negative energy released from feelings of fear will attract more fear, as what you think is what you create.

Acknowledge your fears, release them by lifting up your thoughts and asking for the courage to love and trust. This will transmute those negative energies into positive thoughts which will bring positive results.

Fear is a very physical feeling, for it can pervade your very being. It can start as something small inside you and grow to enormous proportions. Indeed it can take over your life. It will certainly stop you doing, saying, being, what you really want.

Fear is that manifestation of Ego that prevents you from carrying out whatever action you were planning. In some respects it is Ego's defensive tool when you are considering moving away from what Ego says is a safe course.

Fear can get out of hand and rule your life if you are not careful. Then what will happen? Nothing, because you will abandon whatever it was you were planning. When fear takes over, Ego wins. And the more you let fear take over, the more fear will rule your life. But fear needn't be all bad news. Fear recognises that you are facing an unknown, that is, something outwith your experience. Fear is right to kick in and act as a warning in the sense that it should be telling you that you are embarking on something outside your experience to date and you may expect some difficulties, and some learning, but to trust that all will be well. Then let go of that fear and start to trust.

Trust is your Inner Being's recognition that you are setting out on a new venture and telling you that, because you are connected to the Source of all things, all will be well. The boat may rock, but it won't capsize. Trust is the life jacket that keeps you from drowning during the rocky spells. By trusting, you are being positive and showing you know that you will come through your journey safely.

In short, trust will lighten your load, fear will only make it heavier. What you give out you get back. Fear attracts fear, trust in the Universe gets you the trust of the Universe.

Yes, feel the fear, but, having done so, dismiss it and achieve the rewards of trust. The more you trust and are successful, the more you realise you do not need to fear. Don't be pulled down by fearing, soar high by trusting.

When fear takes over, Ego wins.

To what extent are you prepared to let go of fear and trust in the Universe?

What steps could you take right now?

Where do you put your trust – in your Ego or in your Higher Self?

6. Seek and ye shall find: therefore seek only good

Focus your thoughts and attention on something and you will attract it to you. Thoughts are energy and are very powerful. If you think or worry about something, you are putting energy into what you don't want, and you are giving birth to what you really wish to avoid. Focus on what you desire. Use your power of visualisation, use positive affirmations and imagine that what you desire is already part of you. Ask your Higher Self for direction and guidance.

Allow the creative part of you to bring forth what you really want and what is beneficial to you spiritually. Instead of blaming others for your difficulties take responsibility for your life and you will be able to congratulate yourself for bringing forth what you really desire.

In your relationships with others look for the good within them. Everyone has good points. Do not criticise or judge. If you do so, you will be focussing on qualities which will expose themselves to you. Seek out the good in others and you won't be disappointed.

You can find almost anything you want in your modern world. The resources are many and are becoming more accessible to everyone. What was once the realm of the privileged few is now the domain of anyone who seeks. In your world it is not very hard to find some information on any subject: it's almost as if it is at your fingertips. In some cases this is literally where the information lies.

However, having found the information, you have to read, process and decipher it. You have to make judgments on it. Is it what you want? Do you think it is correct? Do you need to search further?

There is so much information available that seeking what you are looking for can become a daunting task and it is easy to feel confused by what you find. It is for you to decide what to believe. If you gather conflicting information then in a sense it is easier for you, because you are considering pros and cons, and not just one or the other.

As always, in making considerations, it is helpful to choose the view that is most in keeping with your own life plan. Therefore you should weigh up your new-found information against your current beliefs and consult with your Higher Self. Do not let Ego enter into the decision making process or else you will be thrown aside from your chosen pathway.

You will also be diverted from your journey if you exclude your Higher Self from the process, because your Higher Self is your guiding light and knows where you are headed.

By seeking information and consulting with your Higher Self you will certainly find what's best for you. To do otherwise is to delay your journey to true knowledge.

Allow the creative part of you to bring forth what you really want.

Why not make today a day in which you change any negative thoughts to positive, loving ones. In the evening reflect on the difference this has made.

Look for the good in everyone you meet and note how much better you relate to others.

7. If you truly forgive you won't want to remember.

You often say you have forgiven and indeed it seems like you have and yet, when another problem crops up with the same person, you go over past events remembering all the details that upset you. This adds fuel to the present fire, magnifying the effect and causing grief to be multiplied. You would not bother to bring it to mind if it no longer meant anything.

Deep down there is still hurt which hasn't been released. You haven't completely forgiven and allowed the ties that bind to be cut. The issues that caused upset still linger deep down and surface from time to time.

When you experience a relationship problem you need to learn to forgive in the real sense of the word. Do it with love, unconditional love, and visualise the ties being cut. Link yourself to the person with unconditional love.

As you practise this you will find there is nothing to forgive anyway. The Ego will not tell you there's a problem. You will feel only unconditional love and realise that the situation arose for a learning experience and be grateful for it, blessing the event and the other person involved. It's alright to state your boundaries and what is right for you, but do this with love. Love never fails but harbour negative emotions and you will fail to move on.

We talk of forgive and forget, but how often do we truly forget? Somewhere in the depths of our mind we will record what has happened. We record everything that happens to us, but we never remember a fraction of it. So why do we always seem to remember those events that require our forgiveness?

Could it be that the acts of forgiving and forgetting are tied to each other in some kind of a way that we do not really understand? Could it be that absolute forgiveness is required to achieve forgetfulness? We may think we have forgiven, and sometimes we just say the word, but deep inside we can't have, for that event keeps rearing its head.

When something happens that causes us hurt or offence or similar, it does not help to just dismiss it with a salutary forgiving. We must look for the lesson, the message for us to understand. Once we have found it and understood it, we can then truly forgive. Indeed you may want to thank the messenger.

That takes great courage, but you will have forgiven from the depths of your Being, from your Soul, from your Higher Self. You will have surrounded everything with love and we know that love dissolves all obstacles. Therefore the incident will be forgotten and you will have grown spiritually.

It can be hard treading the spiritual path but the rewards are well worth the effort. Do you really want to live your life remembering all the unpleasant incidents that have occurred?

Love dissolves all obstacles.

Is there someone now or in the past who could benefit from your forgiveness? Remember that by forgiving you benefit as well and can move on.

If you have trouble forgiving think of a time when someone forgave you and how much it meant to you.

8. Every grudge you hold anchors you to the past

What a waste of time and energy dwelling on what cannot be changed. Anger and regret for what has been leads to a build up of more and more unhappiness and ill-health, with nothing achieved. Let go with love and forgiveness, both for yourself and anyone else involved.

Appreciate what you have learned from the experience and move on with positive emotions so that the present can be enjoyable and fruitful. Take each day as it comes and be fully immersed in whatever it holds for you. Take stock at the end of the day.

Look for the lessons to be learned. Let go of the baggage that is weighing you down. Sending love and light to whatever has upset or angered you will ensure you are free tomorrow of any baggage collected during today. Go to sleep in peace, ready to move forward with the break of a new day.

Why would you hold a grudge? Because someone has upset you or caused you pain in an incident that has long gone. What is the point in reliving that incident time and time again? Are you addicted to pain and suffering?

The incident has occurred, the damage has been done. You have had time to heal the wound, but you won't. You are letting your energies leak away to that past incident and the negativity you generate in doing so means that you cannot move onwards and forwards.

You have to let go. You have to close this wound. Was there a message or lesson you could have learned from this incident occurring? Examine it one more time and get your answer, then close it for ever, sealing and binding it with love. Send out forgiveness and then forget it happened.

When you have done this you will have released one of the strands that is holding you in the past. So you can do the same thing for all the other incidents. Release them one by one until you are completely free. Always send light and love.

You will be rewarded by an upliftment in your spirit and, with the knowledge of why these happened, you are fully prepared for moving on.

Let go of the baggage that is weighing you down.

You can't change the past. Negative emotions have a detrimental effect on the physical body and hold you back spiritually. If you are currently holding a grudge or resentment write down how you would benefit by letting it go.

If you are holding a grudge today release it as you write your journal this evening and note the good feelings associated with this positive action.

9. Release resentment and lighten your load

Resentment is the result of a lack of forgiveness. When others act in a way which displeases you or hurts you there is an inability to accept what has taken place and there is a feeling that you are right and the other person is wrong.

This is judgment and a desire to control others' actions. It's alright to prefer others to be different but do not set rules for them to adhere to. Love yourself and do not look to others for approval. Love others as they are and send them love and light in your quiet moments.

Do not hold grudges or resentment but send forgiveness without any expectations of change. By holding on to resentment you are not going to change what has occurred and you are going to mull over these thoughts which can take over your life. By being weighed down by past events your mind will be filled with negative thoughts which hinder your future progress.

Lovingly forgive others no matter how often you have to do so. This is not a sign of weakness on your part. You can still set your limits but do so with love. Drop the baggage from the past and greet the present with love and light. You will have no negativity to weigh you down.

Everyone carries around with them burdens of one sort or another. Ambition, guilt, revenge, anger, fear. These are just some examples. However like any physical burden these only serve to hold us back from our goal of spiritual development.

You would think that ambition would not be considered a burden, but when it takes over your whole life then that is what it is. It's a force that pulls you away from everything else. Like the other examples it can be a negative issue that you need to resolve.

Resentment is like that too. Resentment encapsulates a number of negative ideas like jealousy, anger, fear, an absence of love. Why should you react in this way to another's achievements or successes? Why wish them ill? Many times it has been said that you get back what you give out.

Everyone has the spark of the divine within them. Use that spark to ignite your potential to be a truly spiritual being. Use that spark to generate your light, then let your light shine out for all to see. Instead of harbouring negative feelings, give out light and love. Encourage, praise, wish well. Whoever you direct these feelings to will feel better and you will also.

When the load is light, everyone benefits. Turn your darkness into light and watch the effect. Don't carry an unnecessary burden that will only get heavier the further you carry it. Release your negative feelings and replace them with positive ones. Positives do not weigh anything at all so you can carry much more than you ever imagined. No burdens, only light. Isn't that wonderful?

> **Drop the baggage from the past and greet the present with love and light.**
>
> What causes you to resent what others have said, done or achieved?
>
> Can you see that by letting go of resentment you free yourself and can make progress?
>
> Do you have expectations of others or can you accept they have free will and you cannot change them?

10. Love is like the tide it has to go in and out

Love is energy and it has to flow to prevent blockages which bring negative circumstances and emotions.

Sending out love to someone even when feelings are fraught can change the entire picture. Close your eyes and send light and love to that person. Accept them as they are. You don't have to agree with what they've done or said, but simply accept them as they are. You can change yourself and your attitudes, but you can't change others or past events. Just send out unconditional love and allow others to find their own way which is right for them. If you feel hurt or angry, release it. It is just your Ego putting up a fight. Allow your Higher Self to take over, and you will realise happiness comes from within and not from others. Remember you get back what you give out.

Some people find it difficult to receive love. It is just as important to accept love as this is part of the flow. Never refuse to accept a kind gesture, a gift or even a smile. When you are faced with a difficult situation and wonder what to do remember love changes everything.

Like lots of other things, love is a two way process. You have to give and receive. This way a balance is maintained and no one person ends up with a monopoly, and no one person ends up with none at all.

By bringing in love and sending it out again you are acting like the tides, and keeping love in motion. Love washes over us as it comes in and when we give it out we expand our being. As we give love out to whoever, wherever or whatever we can see so much more of ourselves, just like the receding water of the tide reveals the land underneath.

But do not think that you have given all of your love out, for you haven't. There is always some retained for your own use. The land under the tidal water does not completely dry out when the tide takes the water out. Use this residual love for your own good. After all before you can love someone else you need to love yourself. Where does this love come from? Yes, the residual love from the tidal flow.

Know also that in giving out love you will also receive love. By being part of the Universal give and take, love is always on the move and the ebbs and flows you help to generate and maintain will ensure that love returns in the next cycle.

The only way you will not receive love in return is by building a barrier, or allowing your channels to silt up. It is therefore important to keep your channels clear, and that requires work on your behalf. Always be aware of what you think, say and do: always be aware of how you treat others.

However you behave affects others, and that in turn affects the flow of love. By being considerate, by being non-judgmental, by being forgiving you are working hard to keep your channels unblocked.

This way love can truly go out and in, and everyone benefits.

Love is a two way process.

Do you find it difficult to love yourself or to accept love?
Why is this?
What changes could you make to enable love to flow in as well as out?

How easy it for you to love others unconditionally?

11. If you give and count the cost you will have to pay the price.

Giving without counting the cost is giving with unconditional love from the heart. It's serving others, and what you give freely will always return. You become hurt and upset when you feel neglected by those to whom you have given so much. If you give grudgingly the price is high, not in monetary terms but in the emotions you suffer as a result: fear, resentment, unhappiness. Just open your heart when you give and make no conditions either verbally to the person or inwardly to yourself. Feel the joy as you are able to share with another.

Trust that no matter what, you can experience love, joy and abundance. You do not have to depend on others to give you these qualities but if you do you will be continually disappointed. Look within to your Spiritual Self, say thanks for what you have, and trust that you will always have your needs met.

Giving and counting the cost doesn't sound like a recipe for a happy existence, because you have placed a monetary value on something that can't be bought or sold. You have let the physical interfere with the spiritual.

Giving is an act of unconditional love and it doesn't matter whether the subject of the giving is physical or spiritual. Giving unconditionally is what you do because you want to, not because you have to.

Counting cost means you are keeping a record – for a reason. Is it to tell everyone how much you gave? Is it to demonstrate your generosity? Whatever it is, it is to reflect well on yourself. Why else would you do it? A gift given in that manner is devalued because it comes with the burden of reluctance. You have given for a reason and that reason was not love, it was obligation. A gift given freely, with love, is so much more valuable because it has been enhanced. It shows in the giver and in the receiver, and will be remembered for a very long time.

The love you give out will go on growing and growing, and it will come full circle back to you. You will receive as you give. Watch faces light up as they appreciate what has been given and how it has been given.

Do not pay the price of negativity by counting the cost of giving. Give with all your heart and with love. That way everyone wins.

If you give grudgingly the price is high.

When did you last give something out of love, unasked, unsolicited?
What feelings did that generate within you?
How did the recipient react?

Do you ever give grudgingly because you think you have no choice?

How do you feel when you believe you have been given something grudgingly?

12. Some people are like the earth -- they need something else to give them light. Be a sun for others.

There are always people who feel low and depressed. Their spirits sink and they feel surrounded by darkness. Most people including yourself have experienced these feelings -- everything seems to go wrong and there is no hope of improvement.

Allow light and love to pour into you, and everything you do will reflect these. Be willing to serve. Be loving, be joyful and caring, and others will receive your light. Remember you can share your light by sending it out during your meditations. Ask to be a channel for healing and light for those in need. You can help others without being in their presence. Think how many candles you could light from just one lit candle, and then think of how many people you could share your light with. Just as each candle that is lit can light many other candles those people to whom you send light can then light the way for others.

The earth is your home, it is where you will live out your physical existence. The planet is immensely varied but provides sufficient products to meet everyone's needs. However, the source of its power to so do is the Sun. For it is the Sun that brings light, warmth and life to earth. No Sun, no physical existence. It really is that simple.

We are all spiritual beings occupying physical bodies, gaining experiences to develop our Souls. Some are aware of this, the vast majority are not. Well, perhaps it is truer to say that the vast majority have forgotten their spiritual dimension. This is not a criticism, for in this physical world there are many things which divert a person's focus. It can be too easy at times to get caught up in the mundane, that is, the everyday events.

We get caught up in events, we get caught up in personal matters, family matters, ambition, rivalry, competition. We get so embroiled we forget who we are and what it is we came to experience. We came here with an agenda and free will, and we have lost one and given the other away.

Those who have remembered or rediscovered their spiritual mission need to set an example for others. They need to be leaders. They need to be like the Sun and bring light and life to those whose spiritual mission is forgotten or unknown.

Show by your thoughts, words and deeds what it is that everyone can be doing. Give out light, give out love. Be a comforter, do not judge. Look for the best in others, give of your best at all times. Most of all be humble and never try to impose yourself or your thoughts on anyone.

The sun shines on everyone on earth without bias or compulsion. You do what you will with sunshine – accept it or repel it. Some like to bask in it, others to hide themselves from it. Each gets according to their needs and free will.

So it should be with you. Do as the sun does. Shine out but don't expect everyone to actively enjoy it. People will react in various ways to you. Do not make judgments and do not set expectations. Shine, and be happy that you are doing your best.

Ask to be a channel for healing and light for those in need.

In what ways can you shine for others?

In your meditation take a few moments to send out love and healing to people and places around the world which could benefit from this.

13. You can only increase your happiness by sharing it.

Everything is energy and energy is constantly moving. Happiness like any other energy such as love, has to keep moving to avoid becoming blocked. You can't keep happiness for yourself: this is selfishness and leads to a diminishing amount, and eventually none.

Give out happiness and, as you share it, it will return many times to you. Feel your happiness and allow it to radiate out to those who need it. This doesn't mean you bounce about in a happy state when someone is overcome with sadness. However, your calmness and love can raise their mood and eventually they will be able to feel happy again.

The only way to happiness is by being satisfied with any situation you are in, knowing that everything has a purpose and comes at the right moment. At an unconscious level your Soul has chosen what is right for you. You need to be in touch with your Soul.

Accept what you have chosen at a higher level. Be in the experience. Be happy and know that whatever comes to you is perfect for your development. We create our own reality. Choose to be happy. Realise no one can make you happy except yourself. Feel this positive energy within and allow others to feel this positive energy radiating from you.

Do not look outside of yourself for a reason to be happy. Acceptance brings joy and the positive energy you radiate will assist in dissipating negative energy within others and they in turn will radiate joy back to you.

Happiness is such by nature that when you experience it you automatically want to share it. It's one of these things you don't want to keep to yourself. Indeed you can't hide it. Anyway, who would want to pretend to be miserable, sad, depressed when the opposite is true? It just doesn't bear thinking about!

Everyone can see you are happy and when you tell them why you are so, it brightens up their lives as well. They become happy for you and everyone benefits.

It's one instance where what you give out comes back tenfold almost instantly. You can see and feel it as it spreads round a room or wherever.

Isn't the world a better place when there's a smile on every face. If only it could be like this all the time. It can be if we all try. We have so much to be happy about that to be otherwise seems almost impossible. Just take a little time to look around you.

Whenever you feel your mood swinging towards sadness think of all the reasons why you should be happy. Share your good fortune with others, share your happiness. You will find others will do the same. No one likes a long face, that's why we share happiness. And, as if by some magical means the happiness doesn't diminish, it grows. One smile can launch so many more. Try it and see.

Choose to be happy.

Have you ever sat down and listed all the things that make you happy?

To what extent do you believe you can change your feelings and emotions?

Choose positive emotions today and note in your journal how this affects your relationship with others.

14. Take a few minutes each day to use all of your senses. You'll find out just what you've been missing.

There are times when you find it difficult to switch off from problems. It's as if you always have to have one on your mind. As soon as one gets resolved another pops up to keep your mind busy. Learn to appreciate the beauty around you and give your mind a rest. Your worries and problems will shrink instead of being magnified by the mind. Whether you are sitting down (and you don't do this enough) or walking along the street, take time to bring your senses to the fore. They don't get a chance most of the time so make sure you allow them to operate. It's amazing what you will notice: the surface you walk on, the flowers in gardens, a person who needs help or just a smile. Use all of your senses and your outlook on life will change.

Using your senses will bring awareness of the beauty of the earth and put you back in touch with nature. It will remind you of the interconnection of all life, and as you uplift your thoughts you will be able to get a clearer perspective of whatever had previously been on your mind.

How often do you really use all of your senses? You look but do you see? You listen but do you hear? What of your other senses? How often do you really use them? Our guess is that you use your senses, but only at a superficial level. You have an awareness of them and that's it.

There is more to your senses than you realise, and it would surprise you what you would find if only you took time to make full use of them.

On the physical plane, in normal daily life it seems to be talk, talk, talk. Everyone can talk, sometimes endlessly. What about the person you are talking to? Are they listening? They most likely can hear you but are they switched on to your message? Do they understand what you are trying to communicate? Are you listening when they reply?

Similarly when you look at something, do you just see what's on the surface, or is there something deeper? If we said "picture a rose" what, actually, would you "see"?

Your sense of smell is perhaps better used, for there is a more direct "assault" on it. You know when something doesn't smell right, like burning or pungency, but do you also react instantly to the more pleasant aromas?

When eating what do you experience? Do you really taste all the different ingredients or is your food covered in condiments for no good reason other than to hide the taste of the underlying food?

Again, when you touch something do you really feel? Can you distinguish textures. Do you just reach out superficially and make a quick judgment?

As we have said earlier, physical life lived at a hurried pace is depriving each one of you of natural pleasures. Take time to use senses at a deeper level and you will uncover a whole new world. You may even uncover new truths, new insights. You may discover new things about yourself.

Even the silence has sounds, even in the darkness you can still see. Also in the darkness you can heighten your sense of touch, in the silence your hearing becomes more accentuated.

How often do you really use all of your senses?

Even walking to work or to the shops is an opportunity to use your senses.
What have you been missing by not using your senses to their fullest capacity?

When you sit down to eat make it a meditation and treat your food with respect. Someone, it might even be yourself, has taken time to prepare it for you. In your meal meditation see, touch, taste, smell.

15. When your world caves in let your spirit rise up

When you experience hurts, sadness, ill health, let downs, a feeling of isolation creeps in. You feel deserted and unsupported. Your world collapses and it's as if you are being sucked into the mire and unable to climb out. These events seem to have no end and no solution. This is due to the fact that your mind is absorbed with thoughts about them instead of seeking answers at a Soul level. It is loss of connection at a Soul level that makes these events seem insurmountable.

Set your problems aside, close your eyes and go into the silence. Say a prayer, raise up your thoughts to your Soul and keep the mind still. With each breath fill yourself with love. Sometimes an answer will be given to you during this time and at other times answers may come at unexpected times and in unexpected ways.

When you come out of the silence radiate the love you have taken in to the situation that worried you. Love it for what it teaches you. Everything comes to teach us something -- maybe patience, trust, tolerance. If all the situation did was to remind you to connect to your Soul then it served a purpose.

It has become a usual practice for us to let our spirit drop when something unexpected or dreadful has occurred. It's as if the event knocks our very being out of our body. We feel devastated, crippled by fear and unknowing. In such times too there are those who can carry on regardless, indeed they seem to thrive on what has happened.

And what has happened? They have allowed their spirit to rise rather than fall. They have allowed their Inner Self to shine through and are able to navigate a positive way forward.

How do they manage? It's a good question, but inside they "know" that the event is a learning experience. They allow themselves to be guided by Inner Senses. They trust their feelings, they trust their Higher Self.

You too can learn to do this. Time and application are all you need. Sit quietly and let the physical world around you disappear into nothingness. You may still hear the sounds of the world, but they will be distant and not disturb you.

In your spiritual dimension you will find your Higher Self – your Inner Being. Your Higher Self is there to guide you, not to control you. Seek and you will find your intuition. You can communicate with your Self, and will undoubtedly be surprised at some of the answers you receive.

By taking time to communicate you will learn to trust the answers for they are given to help you realise your objectives, to achieve the goals you set before you incarnated. Your Inner Being will not deceive: it cannot.

When you have learned to trust the advice that has been given you will surely make spiritual progress, for you will certainly be walking the pathway you identified before you were born.

You will thus be raising your spirit, and you will be doing it every day, in every way, and not just waiting for the moment when your world caves in. By raising your spirit at every opportunity you may find that your world will never cave in.

Your Higher Self is there to guide you, not to control you.

Make time to sit in the quiet and contact your Higher Self. Express your concerns, ask for guidance then detach from the outcome. You will be surprised at how your concerns are taken care of.

Regular quiet times connecting with your Higher Self help to ensure you can cope with whatever confronts you. Are you making time daily for this?

16. If you love everything that occurs you will have nothing to complain about

If you truly love everything you are not setting standards, demands or expectations. You accept whatever comes to you. You accept everyone irrespective of their thoughts, actions, beliefs. This doesn't mean you agree with how they act but it does mean you recognise that on the inside there is a divine spark in others, just as there is within you.

You understand that others are on a journey like yourself, that they have to take responsibility for themselves and that they are not infallible. Love them as they are, without trying to change them.

By accepting people and events in a loving way you will not be frustrated with a desire to attempt to change what you cannot.

You will experience serenity and peace and contentment which you would not experience if you were to complain and desire to control.

By lovingly accepting all things you are aware that there is a purpose in everything and the God in you will be acknowledging the God within all people.

When things get on top of us, when something doesn't go as we'd hoped or expected we become very disappointed and let down. This feeling is very quickly followed by the rush to complain about what's gone wrong. When we do this we are on the attack. Our sense of anger, injustice, whatever you want to call it is heightened and off we go with all guns blazing.

Very often we don't stop to wonder why the matter has developed as it has. We don't know what circumstances led to the "wrong" outcome.

How often has your complaint led to further frustration as your anger has controlled your actions and your pride won't let you take any other course but that which your anger has demanded? You allow yourself to get into conflict. This almost encourages the wrong outcome to your complaint.

When things go wrong, as they do, and as they will, would it not be better to take an initial step back instead of forwards and look at what has occurred? You can then see the possible reasons why the outcome has turned out this way. Look on the matter with love and treat it as a learning experience. Everything that happens does so for a reason and there is a lesson for someone in each event.

When we control our aggressive nature the world seems to be a better place. Of course it is! No Egos fighting each other for dominance. No reason to escalate the situation beyond redemption as sometimes happens. Just plain common sense settling the differences and mending fences, not destroying them.

In the calmness love will prevail. In a loving situation resolution can be found. A life less fraught can be yours if only you will change your attitude. Swap aggression for love and see your life change for the better.

By lovingly accepting all things you are aware that there is a purpose in everything.

Is there a difficult situation now which upsets you? If so, how could you benefit by appreciating the lessons it presents?

Do you feel able to thank the Universe for what you are gaining spiritually from such situations?

17. Never be jealous. If you don't have it you don't need it

If you believe your needs are not being met then they won't be. This is the thought you are sending out to the Universe and this is the way things will be. When you feel you are lacking in anything it is easy to be jealous of others who appear to have what you think you need.

Examine what you have and see everything as a gift. Value everything you have instead of putting value on what you think you lack.

Believe you are abundant and that all your needs are fully met. The positive thoughts you are sending out will allow the Universe to maintain your abundance. Whatever you have will be sufficient for you. You will know that whatever you don't have is not necessary and indeed by not having it you are learning something you would not otherwise learn. Allow others the pleasure of having whatever they have and allow yourself the same pleasure.

Why is it you look on something someone else has and immediately want it for yourself? What is it about you that turns you into someone who wants what others have? It's your Ego. Your Ego tells you that you need the material item or lifestyle of someone else.

Your Ego identifies physical things such as possessions or good looks – however you define these – as symbols of achievement. Without them you cannot be the success you so want to be.

So, in its bid to get these so called trappings of success for you, your Ego plants the thoughts that you need them, and, that until you get them, you will be a no-hoper, an underachiever.

The thoughts play on your emotions and you find yourself more and more bitter and twisted as envy takes over. Every time you see the "symbols of success" jealousy fills your entire Being and you become consumed with negativity.

You will find that your relationships with those you envy will deteriorate. You will find yourself speaking ill of them too, especially when they are not present to defend themselves. The negative passion of your jealousy will eat away at you and you will be completely distracted from what you could be doing. Why be jealous? Will it really enrich your life if you had everything you desire? Or would you merely find that the more you have the more you want?

The Universe is abundant. That means that everything you need you already have or will have at the correct time. Indeed right now you probably have more than you need. How often do you use everything you possess? How much do you have in cupboards and attics that has not seen the light of day for many years? Most people are in this situation yet they perceive themselves as lacking. Ego tells them they need more than they have. Ego wants and Ego persists until Ego gets. You let Ego drive you to places you really don't need to go to.

Really it would be better to consult your Self when Ego makes demands. Bypass Ego and consult your Inner Self because only your Inner Self really knows what it is you need. It is your Inner Self that remembers why you adopted this physical body and lifestyle. It knows who you really are and what's right for you.

Frequent and regular communication will tell you if and when Ego is right, for Inner Self does not lie or make demands. Inner Self will keep you free from jealousy and in this freedom you will come to realise that what others have and what they seem to be is for them alone: your success will depend on whether or not you are trying to achieve the goals you set yourself before you were born.

Examine what you have and see everything as a gift.

Make a list of everything you have and realise how much your needs are already met.

Jealousy is a negative emotion which deters progress. Is there something you feel that someone else has that you don't have in your life right now? If so, do you really need it? If not, could your thoughts be channelled in a more positive direction?

18. You don't know how rich you are until you count your blessings

When you lose connection with your Higher Self you find your world begins to fall in and you become tearful and despondent. It's as if you have no joy and the joys that once filled your heart now mean nothing and seem only to give painful memories.

You become filled with sadness, blaming others for your grief and 'if only' seems to be the start of every internal sentence you speak. If you could only stay connected and from a higher point of view see your whole situations and events past and present.

When looking at events and people from a higher perspective everything is seen in a different light. You allow your own light to shine and you see the light in others also. You realise they are beautiful spirits in physical bodies going through experiences like yourself.

You realise the connection you all have to Source and see beauty and love everywhere. You become grateful for the past and appreciate the present as well.

All people, all situations have a purpose and as you appreciate everything, you become thankful for them. Every moment of every day becomes a blessing, an opportunity for growth, an opportunity to serve and love.

There's no need for tears, no reason to apportion blame, no need for self-pity, no need for anger, and no need for jealousy or fear for the future. Everything is a blessing.

This is abundance with all needs being met in whatever way is right for you. The wise man knows he is rich: the man who loses his spiritual connection is always poor.

Human nature is such that in general terms, the vast majority always look at life from the negative side or angle. Always, or so it seems to us, the concentration, the focus, is on what we don't have. We are very good at itemising what's missing from our existence. We are experts at composing wish lists of "must haves", items, yes material objects, that would make our lives a joy to live.

But would they? Chances are that if our wish list was somehow magically fulfilled we would find that it actually wasn't complete at all. There would be other things that would need to be added to it. And so on it goes, never reaching true fulfilment, never reaching true happiness.

But what of the things we actually have, either as personal items, or as those we have access to? Do you ever stop to think about all the things you take for granted? If you started to list these items you would spend some considerable time doing so, for there are a great number of them. Try it and see for yourself.

If the items, which you take for granted, were not there your life would be affected in such a huge way that you would perhaps be devastated. Look at the list. What does it contain? Can you buy these items? Certainly not! What price would you ever put on a smile, or on an act of unconditional love? It is impossible, because these things are above a monetary value.

Your life is what you make of it, and the Universe in its wisdom has provided you with all the ingredients you need to make you happy, successful and have a fulfilled life. So what is stopping you from achieving it? Competition? Greed? Do you really think lots of money and expensive possessions bring happiness? What if your health suffers in the process?

No, my friends, lots of money doesn't bring fulfilment. Inside, your Higher Self knows what brings this, but how often do you consult with your Inner Being?

Take some time each day to go inside and make contact. Reflect on what has gone before and what the lessons have been. Review in conjunction with your Higher Self, who you are and what it is you are looking for.

Compare your answers to your list of taken-for-granted items and you will see that fulfilment is yours for the taking. Grasp it joyfully with both hands.

The wise man knows he is rich: the man who loses his spiritual connection is always poor.

What do you value that you can't buy?

Each day send out gratitude to the Universe for all that you have.

19. You can be your own best friend or your own worst enemy. What would you rather choose?

You have learned much about the above from your personal experiences. Unfortunately many people have still to learn how much they create their experiences and how they have the power to be responsible for their feelings and wellbeing.

Your reactions to others and to circumstances is so important. When you remember to give love, unconditional love, to all and to circumstances that present themselves, you realise that peace, joy and love are yours.

By choosing to accept what comes your way and knowing that all things work together for the good of all, you have the peace of mind, the reassurance that all will be well. That is a gift to yourself. That is being your own best friend.

By choosing otherwise, such as facing adversity with anger, jealousy, fear, frustration, you become bitter and resentful and your mind is filled with thoughts that cause you pain. You are attacking yourself and you are nothing more than your worst enemy.

Take a moment to reflect on this when faced with difficult situations. Choose your reactions wisely, give out unconditional love and you will not only be your own best friend but a best friend to others as well.

It is said that enemies can teach us many things about ourselves. Indeed it is said that enemies are perhaps the best teachers we could ever have. However this is not an exhortation to go out and make enemies with everyone you meet. You need friends too!

The thing is, though, that if you make yourself your enemy you won't learn a thing. By turning yourself into your worst enemy you will destroy your life. You will fill your entire being with such amounts of negativity that you may even lose your health, both physical and mental.

You will pick up on everything that you think, do or say in an over critical way and will dissect yourself in great detail. You will only succeed in heaping pain upon pain, tragedy upon tragedy.

You will live in the negative. You will radiate negativity to all and sundry. The Universe will pick up on this and return it to you in abundance. There is a great chance you may lose your friends and be shunned by family. Your employment will suffer, your career may disappear.

If that's what you want then that's your choice because you have free will and you can choose to do whatever you like.

However, before you make that choice, consider another option: that of befriending yourself. It may be a harder road to follow but it is more rewarding. Just think what it would be like to love yourself and everything you did. You could live the life you chose for yourself before birth. You could achieve your spiritual goals.

You have to take time to get to know yourself: real friends don't just appear in an instant. You need to make contact with the Inner You, and remain in communication.

Find out what it is you opted to achieve in this lifetime. Find out what it is you really like and are comfortable with: not someone else's choice for you. Find out what makes you tick. Discover where you really want to go, discover who you really are.

You will be surprised at the answers, but they are true, for your Inner Self tells no lies. It is your guardian, it is your guide. Your Inner Self will tell you just how you really are. No Ego to satisfy, just straight talking.

Once you have made friends with yourself, and love yourself for what you are, you can then set about loving others. You will radiate positivity to all and sundry and the Universe will return this to you in abundance.

Imagine the happiness, the love, the self-confidence. Wouldn't it be wonderful to know that you are treading your spiritual path, radiating like a beacon of love, an example for others to see and follow (if that is their choice).

We have shown you two options: which one do you think fits your life plan best?

Choose your reactions wisely.

List ten things you like about yourself. This can include physical attributes, characteristics, etc.

Name five positive qualities you possess.

Is anything stopping you from being your own best friend?

When you react negatively to others what are the consequences?

20. Take control of the present for once it becomes the past you've lost control of it for ever

Fear leads to loss of control. You begin to worry, you become upset and your mind runs riot. We are here to remind you that we are available to support and guide you if you will only ask. The way to be in control is to switch off the conscious mind, be still and allow help to flow through. Being in control is not about controlling others. It's about taking the right decision for the highest good of all.

If your mind is cluttered with fearful emotions you cannot get clear ideas as to the right outcome. This leads to saying things and doing things you may later regret and cannot change. You then live with regret and remorse wishing you could go back and change things, but of course it's too late.

No matter what is happening we want you to make time for these quiet moments. They are even more important when things seem to be going differently from what you would wish. Still the mind, ask for clarity and you will be in a position to take the right action.

You will be able to progress knowing that the past actions were what seemed right for you at that time and you will not waste time regretting what can't be changed.

Your thoughts all manifest in the Now. You can't think in the Past and you don't know what you will think tomorrow, or in an hour's time for that matter. Thoughts are always of the moment.

With this realisation and the knowledge already stated many times before that your thoughts are your reality, you need to come to terms with the idea that you have responsibility for them. Control your thoughts and you control your reality. You control what you think, say and do.

Everything you do is done in the present. It all happens now. Your whole reality lasts for the moment and then becomes your past. When it becomes your past you have lost control because the chance has gone.

You simply cannot change the past. If you are not happy with your past you cannot change it. You can try, in the here and now, to make amends, to take actions to try to right a wrong, but you cannot alter the original act. It has been done or said.

Live for the moment, live for the present. Be responsible for what you do. By taking control you will always be happy with your actions and have no regrets when you look back, as everyone does from time to time.

It is not to say your life will be perfect, but when you look back you will see what you have to learn more clearly. The love and light you give out will return to you as the energies move around. Give out, get back. A little control now means much joy later. It is a glorious cycle, be part of it.

Control your thoughts and you control your reality.

Take time throughout the day to monitor your thoughts. Be willing to change negative thoughts into positive ones and note the difference this makes.

How does it feel to be in control of your own reality? Does this make you feel empowered or do you dislike the responsibility?

21. Your batteries are only as good as what they're charged with.

When your energy becomes low negative thoughts and fears creep in. You know you are not achieving your full potential. Only you have control over this. If you allow your energies to drop you become despondent, lethargic and achieve very little.

The onus rests with you. It is your choice to allow your batteries to run out or to keep them topped up. The lower they get the more difficult it is to get them fully operational again.

You have to be disciplined and set aside time for growth. It can be reading a book or an article (you will usually find the right one pops up when needed) or taking time to be still and asking for replenishment.

You then become focussed on what you really want and it's amazing what you achieve and how everything falls into place. Never see this time as wasted. It's a time of recharging, enabling you to move on instead of seeing progress diminish or even cease. Access positive energy and enthusiasm which you can then project into the Universe: others can benefit from this.

Your strength comes from within. You cannot look outside of yourself for energy. All is inside and you have to use every means available to tap and unlock this energy. Flat batteries give out nothing and are useless for power. They need to be charged and the energy flows from the battery to whatever is to be activated.

You need to replenish continually as energy is used up. Regular healthy eating, not overeating but just enough of the essentials. Sleep has to be adequate otherwise you become lethargic and there is nothing to drive you. Thoughts are energy. Put the right thoughts in your mind and you will benefit from these. Negative thoughts will produce nothing helpful and will drag you down. Spend time relaxing and meditating. Be open to receiving wisdom and put this into practice.

You can only give out what you have. It is obvious to say that what you don't have you can't give. So you can't give out love if you don't have love within you.

Your batteries are, if you like, what make you work. They are your power source and allow you to do what you have to do. Recharge them with low grade fuel and they will allow you to work at a low level, and not for very long. You will spend much time recharging and will be unable to live life to the full.

Also, what you give out comes back to you. So if you are sending out low level energy that's what will return to you. Round and round the spiral you will go, but it will be a spiralling downwards not upwards.

To move upwards, that is to achieve your spiritual goals, you will need to raise your energy levels. With better fuel you will be able to reach higher and higher, your energy will reach out further. The spiralling is therefore not only upwards, but outwards too. Receiving as you give means a constant increase in your energy levels.

How can you increase the quality of your energy? For the answer you need to consult your Inner Being, your Higher Self. You will certainly need to consider how you live your life: what is important to you, what you must do and what you must do to achieve those objectives.

Are you prone to anger quickly? Are you selfish, thinking only of yourself? Are you judgmental? Do you make quick decisions without knowing or wanting to know all the facts? Can you forgive? And forget? Do you send out unconditional love to all and everyone?

These are just some of the questions you need to ask yourself and, in conjunction with your Higher Self decide on a way forward. Take small steps: all journeys begin with small steps. That way you will be encouraged to stay with the plan, for chances are the small steps will bring small successes. Biting off more than you can chew can bring disappointment and you may be put off continuing. Remember that everything of any size can be broken down into smaller units.

One success will lead to another and your change of lifestyle will be gradual. You will find your energy changing as you do. Changing direction can be a difficult thing to do, but with commitment, and frequent conversations with your Inner Being, you will achieve those spiritual goals you set and you will find that your batteries will be charged with fuel of the highest quality.

You have to be disciplined and set aside time for growth.

In what ways can you manage your time more efficiently to get the quality time you need for your Spiritual growth?

How well do you take care of your physical body? Remember all our bodies, physical, mental, emotional and spiritual, need to be balanced for us to operate at an optimum level.

22. Strength is something you don't know you have until you need it

How often have you come through a difficult or painful situation and, looking back, you wondered how you managed to cope. You realised you coped admirably and were able to support others as well. We are always with you and we do our best to assist you at all times. It is important that you want help. We won't force assistance on you if it is not what you desire. We suggest you do not wait until a major crisis before asking for help.

Take time daily to look at your current situation and ask for strength to get through. You can call on us and we will welcome your requests. We are not here to take away situations but to support you in your growth and learning.

By asking for help you are acknowledging that there is an issue to be dealt with and this is much better than ignoring it and hoping it will disappear. The sooner you accept it and ask for guidance the sooner it will pass. Know your needs, ask for help and you will know your strength.

It's amazing what people discover about themselves when faced with adversity or a difficult situation. It is generally the worst of situations that brings out the best in people. Isn't that a strange thing?

It appears that when the situation seems doomed, we remember something we never knew we had forgotten, or display a trait we thought was absent.

It's not just brute strength that is meant here. Yes, there are countless incidents of demonstrations of previously undisplayed physical strength in life threatening situations.

Strength of character is meant too. Incidents occur seemingly all at once or one after the other in rapid succession. These incidents would be bad enough on their own, however their effect is compounded by their frequency. In such situations we find an inner strength that carries us through.

The inner strength stems from our connection to Source. It is the Universe helping us along our spiritual pathway. There is a reason for everything and that inner strength helps us to identify the lessons and messages. When we have trust in the Universe we can stand tall in crises.

Sometimes it takes a crisis to teach us to go within and find our Inner Self. And when we have done so we learn to trust what it says. We can help ourselves by not waiting for a crisis to find our Inner Self: we can actively seek it, and, once found, constantly converse with it.

When you are in contact with your Inner Self you will find out more about yourself and so it won't only be strength you have found, but everything you need to achieve your spiritual goals.

When we have trust in the Universe we can stand tall in crises.

What insights have you discovered about yourself?

Regular contact with your Higher Self enables you to trust that the Universe will give you the strength you need in order to deal with whatever situations confront you.
How regular is your contact?

What activities give you more inner strength?
Do you use these regularly or only in times of crisis?

23. Go within and you won't go without

Your true needs will not be met by keeping your thoughts at a physical level. If you do this you will always imagine you never have enough and feel poor. Indeed you will be poor in spirit as this part of your life will be neglected.

Control your life from the highest level possible. This means taking time to connect to your Higher Self as it is your Higher Self that knows your purpose in life and your requirements to fulfil this purpose you chose prior to incarnating. Connect each day by going within and upwards. Indicate your willingness to serve Source and your needs will be met to allow you to do this.

When you are on your right pathway and working on a love vibration you will feel balance and harmony in all you do, and whatever you need will appear at the right time and in the right way.

Sometimes you may perceive the world as a place without love, a place without pity. A cruel place that brings nothing but trouble and bad times. Why should this be so? At these times did you bother to ask what your contribution was? Possibly you asked "Why me?" but did you listen for an answer? Very often our communication is a one-way channel. Ask, ask, ask, but never listen.

We ask in a way that suggests that whoever hears will sort it out without further input from ourselves. Actually you get back what you give out. You are responsible for yourself. You are responsible too for ensuring that anything you do is not at the expense of others.

So in these times of darkness, we advise going within. We all lose connection with our own being, sometimes short-lived, sometimes it is more permanent. There are times when things seem to be going well and we lose that connection, quickly forgetting why everything is so good.

Inside you will find the real you. Inside you will discover wisdom and unconditional love. Go inside and make contact. When you have established contact stay in touch. Don't let it get to the stage of your Inner Being being someone you used to know but somehow you drifted apart.

The time is now when the planet is moving upwards in terms of vibration and everyone on it needs to do so too, or be left behind. If you truly are seeking the spiritual goal then going inside and establishing two-way communication is the start.

Take that small step: it is not difficult, and help is always available. When you have done so, you know your journey has started, and each time you go inside, you know your journey continues in the right direction.

Control your life from the highest level possible.

Are you keeping a journal of your quiet times and recording such things as what your concerns were, what insights you received or what advice you were given?

Do you regularly look to others for guidance?
How successful is this?
Do you go within and check this out with your Higher Self?

24. If you can't see the light you haven't looked beyond the darkness

When problems beset us it is easy to believe everything is against us and we cannot see beyond the current circumstances. The mind becomes absorbed in thoughts about our trials and all seems doom and gloom with no light at the end of the tunnel. It's in circumstances like this that we need to take time to be still and raise up our thoughts.

This is easier said than done but if we practise this when things are going well it will be much easier to do when times and circumstances are difficult. Through practice you realise the benefits to be derived from these quiet moments and know that help is available when requested. It doesn't mean difficulties are lifted away but it does make us open to receiving ideas and inspiration to get through them.

Rise up in your thoughts to the level of light and know that the darkness of physical circumstances can be a factor that leads you to walk closer to your Higher Self.

We all have periods of darkness. Periods when we think all is lost or the world is against us. Our spirit is very low at these times and we almost abandon all hope. We seem to stumble from one crisis to another. Often our health deteriorates.

In these dreadful times all we are aware of is the darkness. All we see is the darkness. It surrounds us, it prevents us from reaching where we'd like to be.

But if you sit in the darkness and do nothing that is exactly what you will achieve. If you look you will find that you can still see. There is no darkness so intense that you cannot move for fear of danger. There may be times when it is better not to move, but you will still be able to see.

The light is there! It is the light, no matter how dim, no matter how diffuse, that pervades everything. If you concentrate on the light it will get brighter. As it gets brighter the darkness will dissipate and you will again be where you want to be. From being lost you will be found.

Remember this in your darkest moments. There is always someone wanting to help you. Help often comes from strange and unexpected places. Often the person who brightens the light is someone previously unknown.

Always reach for the light for it will never harm you. In the light you will always know where you are, and sometimes the bringer of the light will demonstrate in a positive fashion who your friends really are.

The darkness is not all bad, but only so if you do not look for the message or learn the lesson. The Universe is always sending us messages and does so in many ways. The Universe also sends us the answers to our questions and problems. We have to look for them. We have to look for them beyond the darkness our Ego surrounds us with. We have to look for the light.

The Universe is always sending us messages.

When you experience a period of darkness, still yourself, close your eyes and go inwards. Ask for help and guidance from your Higher Self, the Angels and other Beings of Light. Notice how the light shines down on you, bringing you peace and hope.

Do you believe there is something positive in all situations?

25. Think before you speak: you may want to change your thoughts.

It is good to get into the habit of monitoring your thoughts. It is easy to come up with a thought and immediately put it into spoken words which you later regret. Once angry and hurtful words have been spoken they cannot be undone. Always be aware of the power of thoughts whether they become spoken or not. The negative energy they hold is harmful to you and others.

Very often we regret things we have said to others and even when we apologise at a later date the other person may not accept this, causing us despair and unhappiness. When unloving thoughts come into mind be aware of them, cancel them, replacing them with loving, caring thoughts which can then be put into spoken words if appropriate. These thoughts will always have positive outcomes and there will be no regrets or a desire to change what cannot be changed.

Be centred and in control at all times. Take time away from difficult situations or environments in order to ensure your thoughts are of the highest kind. When faced with other people's angry words do not fall into the trap of returning like with like. Be centred in yourself, choosing thoughts which will benefit you both. This takes courage, and you cannot be sure that the other person will respond in the way you'd like. However, ultimately love conquers all and your loving thoughts will give you strength to get through.

Never underestimate the power of thought. If you are happy with your thoughts you will be happy with what you say and do.

We use words to express ourselves. We use them to tell others how we feel, what we want, what we like and so on. We use words to communicate. Fact and fiction would not exist without words. Yes, there are other ways to communicate, but they are not nearly as good or as efficient as words.

Words can be gentle and soothing. Words can be helpful and uplifting. Said or written wrongly they can be devastating and negative.

Harsh words, hurtful words are often spoken in the heat of the moment, uttered without consideration. Therein lies the sorrow, for so much damage can be done to everyone when this happens. It is best to always consider what it is you have to say when the situation calls for it. Thoughts are the basis of reality and if you think a situation through then all will be well and the right words will come out.

When you allow negative emotions to speak for you, you can expect a backlash. Anger provokes anger, hurt provokes self defence. There is a saying "If you can't say anything nice then say nothing", and it is good advice.

When the situation merits it, think before you speak and you will say the right things. There are times when you can say almost anything and cause no harm or upset, but you will know when these are for they are likely to be less serious moments, moments of happiness or humour. The situation will be "light" when you can do this.

It is important to learn the difference, for once you start to use hurtful words in a serious situation when emotions are emerging, you will be stepping on to the slippery downward slope of conflict. A clear head is required in serious situations so make sure you do everything you can to remain in control of your thoughts.

Practise meditation. Practise the art of staying calm. Practise the ways you can get in touch with your Higher Self. Practise the ways to remain in touch with your Inner Being. If you can control your emotions and put Ego to one side then you are well on the way to saying the words that everyone wants to hear.

Never underestimate the power of thought.

How often do you monitor your thoughts throughout the day? Are you prepared to make changes, turning negative into positive? How can you do this?

26. Change your attitude and you will see the world in a different light

You have a saying that refers to looking at a difficult or depressing situation through rose coloured spectacles. The saying infers the person is viewing a situation and being unrealistically optimistic. We would say you don't need to look through rose coloured spectacles to see the beauty in the world.

See from your heart. Let the light shine out and this will project light to all circumstances. The way you think will influence your view. As within so without. If you believe a problem is insurmountable it will be. If you believe others don't like you, you are unlikely to elicit a friendly response from them.

Believe in yourself. Believe in others. Remember they too are beautiful Souls going through the school of life with all its lessons. Take each situation and adopt a positive approach and you will notice the difference: believe that everything works together for good in the end.

As your outlook gets brighter your view of the world will be bright, just like when the clouds drift away, and the sun comes into view. Be filled with light and the world will reflect it back to you.

_____

My child you see your world as it is created by you. Your thoughts are your reality. Your view is tinged by your feelings, your emotions. These affect how you act, how you see, how you think. Your feelings affect what you believe. The world can be many things, the world can be anything. You make it what it is for you.

In creating your view of the world do you ever stop to consult your Inner Self? Maybe deep inside there is a different view that is being suppressed by egotistical feelings. Do you know what these other views might be?

Attitude is how you portray yourself. Your Ego has this view of what you are. It has been fed by countless years of conditioning, by exposure to other people's views of what they would like you to be. You could almost say that your attitude is the result of giving away your free will. Oh yes, your Ego still thinks you are exercising it, but are you? Attitude is seen as an aggressive force and people think that you need "attitude" to tell the world who and what you are. However, if you soften its meaning and use it to describe an aspect of your being then you will manage much better.

Having a positive attitude or a loving attitude means you are displaying the caring and sharing aspects of your being. You can do this without any aggression, for these aspects do not need to be forced out or forced onto anyone else.

Attitude used as an aggressive term is dark and foreboding, for you are trying to force yourself or your views on someone else. It is negative and will ultimately rebound on you. To those expressing "attitude" we say "lighten up" and by that we mean take away the aggression, take away the darkness. Let some light shine on your world. Try going inwards before going outwards. You will see the light and you will see it grow brighter. Lighten up and see the difference.

Be filled with light and the world will reflect it back to you.

How can you soften any aggressive aspects of your character and what benefits will you accrue by doing so?
Put this into practice and note the positive effects in your journal.

27. You cannot judge if you don't have all the facts.

It is easy to judge others, thinking you have all the facts and know best. We like to think we have all the right answers and can't understand why others differ. No one person has access to the truth. Everyone has his or her own understanding and what one perceives to be true one day may be different another day.

At a physical level we cannot know everything that is going on. It is not possible to have all the facts or to understand where another person is coming from. It is not possible to have knowledge of all that they are going through or what issues they are trying to deal with. If someone seems angry or difficult to communicate with, understand that they have problems themselves and their anger may not be intended to be directed at you.

No matter what difficulties appear you will never have the whole picture available for viewing. We are all interconnected and everything happens in the right way and at the right time. Do not judge if something or someone is right or wrong. Take time to send out love knowing that the only way to deal with the matter is at a spiritual level.

Be concerned with what you can learn rather than wanting to control something or someone you can never fully understand. Face the limited facts you have and use them in a loving manner.

The statement is obvious. Until you know all the facts, all the details, you cannot rightly make a decision. Your Common Law is based on this. In a trial one side portrays the evidence in one light and the other side in a different light. However there is an assumption made that all the facts are known.

The Law uses the term "beyond reasonable doubt" and this is sound advice. Be very certain before you judge. For good or bad the advice is the same. A jigsaw cannot be completed if a piece is missing, and who knows what that piece will show?

Control your emotions, control your thoughts and you will see that your inclination to jump in and judge will subside. It is never a race to make a judgment, so slow down and take time to assemble all the pieces. Only when you have the big picture can you deal with the details, for by having the overall view you will know where the details fit.

If you have to make a quick decision ask your Higher Self and go with your intuitive feeling, but always try to find out as much as you can.

Even when you have all the facts the evidence can be portrayed in different ways. Consider the story of the race between the red car and the blue car. It was reported that the blue car finished second whereas the red car finished next to last. This gives an entirely different view of the race!

Facts are strange things. They point you towards the truth but don't necessarily tell the whole truth. Always, you have to decide. But we say to you, gather what you can and judge accordingly. Be prepared to change your view. Better still be non-judgmental.

A jigsaw cannot be completed if a piece is missing.

What causes you to be judgmental?
What steps can you take to eliminate these traits?

Have you ever made a judgment about someone and been proved wrong?
How did this make you feel?

28. Let go of attachments to make room for what is right.

Holding on to things or relationships is the work of the Ego. The Ego likes to control and fears losing this. By holding on you are giving your power away and your happiness depends on keeping these attachments. All your energies are channelled in a direction which may not be right for you or others.

Whatever is right for you will be attracted to you if you allow your Higher Self to direct. This involves having trust to let go of what may no longer serve you and trust that the Universe knows best.

Look carefully at what you are holding on to and fear losing. Ask yourself why you are doing this and what you hope to achieve. Are you doing this for selfish reasons or for the good of everyone involved? Are you operating from unconditional love or conditional love? If you are laying down conditions you are excluding your Higher Self from the decision making. Free yourself from the bonds of attachments. Be free to move forward into new situations and experiences that are beneficial for your spiritual progress.

Attachments bring stagnation, letting go creates space for you to flourish.

There are those ideas, ideals, beliefs and such like that we each hold on to. They are part of our current being. By our very nature we form an attachment to them. Sometimes we know why we have done so, perhaps it has suited our belief system at that point. Similarly there are times when we do not know why we have made an attachment -- it "just happened". There are yet other times when we have been persuaded, yes, even conditioned, to accept that something is right for us.

We have all been there. We have all done that. But did we ever think deeply about what we took on? I would say in some cases we did, but in most cases the decision was largely made for us.

What are your attachments? Do you ever stop to wonder? Do you ever list out your beliefs, principles, whatever, and ask yourself where they came from? Do you ever examine them for relevance to your current situation? Have they contributed to your situation?

It would be of great benefit to examine yourself and see if there is anything you are holding on to that has no relevance to where you are hoping to reach, physically, mentally, emotionally or spiritually.

You probably change your car or computer every few years, so why don't you give yourself a service too. You may be surprised at what you are carrying around in your being. Perhaps you need to make adjustments, update your system. It may be that old ideas are holding you back.

Spring clean your outlook and see what needs to change. After all your clothes come into and go out of fashion, but you have no problem changing them around. Extend the idea to include the inner you. It is time to have a clear out to make room for new ideas, new beliefs. Don't just drop the old like a hot potato, release it with love -- it was part of you after all.

Attachments bring stagnation, letting go creates space for you to flourish.

To what extent do your actions demonstrate your beliefs?

To what extent are you attached to particular outcomes? Remember these may not serve your Highest Good.

Are you willing to trust that your Higher Self knows more about what is right for you than your Ego? Are you willing to let go and trust?

29. Operate from the heart but remember the fuel it needs is love.

You cannot go wrong if you operate on a love vibration. Open up your heart centre and allow love to flow out to all individuals and to all situations. Give out unconditional love and do not judge. You can never fully understand where others are coming from or why certain situations confront you. Remember to look for the Divine in everyone, knowing that all life is one.

If you find a relationship or a situation difficult to handle, visualise love going from your heart centre to where it is needed. Let love do the healing. Remember you get back what you give out. Love can turn situations around and this benefits all who are involved.

If you allow the Ego to direct you, you will find all sorts of reasons for not giving out love. Never view giving out love as a sign of weakness. It takes strength to shut out the Ego, to be non-judgmental and loving no matter what. The Ego fears failure but with love there can be no failure. You may not always get the results you would prefer but love all events knowing that they are right for you at that particular time.

If you operate from the heart you will be listening to the guidance from your Soul which will be exactly what is needed at that particular time.

––––––––––––––––––––––––––

We often talk about the heart of something meaning its very being. So too with your body, because, of all the vital organs, the heart is the most important. From before you are born until you die it will beat with a rhythm that keeps the blood flowing round the rest of the body. With the blood comes the nutrients that keep us alive.

The heart is also a symbol of love. It is said that the heart is the centre of true love, and when we get hurt we are said to be broken hearted. The hurt can spread through not just our physical body, but the other bodies too, particularly the emotional body.

Sometimes too, we hear of people allowing the heart to rule the head meaning they haven't applied due and proper care to their decision making. However, we can operate from the heart, so long as we act in love. The head can be cold and calculating, but not the heart. When we send out unconditional love we are never looking for profit or return.

We are sending out an energy that is positive and uplifting in the hope that others will respond with joy and, in their turn, pass out more. It is true that love can make the world go round. It would be absolute joy if love were to go round the world. Imagine how it would feel.

Fill your heart with love. See the positive everywhere you go and in everything you do. Take pleasure in every act you perform. Then give it all out to the world, to the Universe. Watch as it goes out. Take note of what happens. And take note too of that love returning to you. You have to give in order to receive, it is true, so give out that which you would most like to receive.

The Ego fears failure but with love there can be no failure.

We can't truly love others if we have a problem loving ourselves. What steps can you take to ensure that you like who you are and what you do?

Is there a current relationship which is upsetting you in some way?
Are you willing to release hurt, anger or any other negative emotion and send out unconditional love, trusting that the outcome will be for the highest good of all involved?

30. Nourish your mind as well as your body.

It is important to do your best to maintain your physical health. This means having the right amount of sleep, exercise and nourishing food to maintain the fitness of your physical body. However this is only part of the means to health. It is easy to become obsessed with physical fitness and omit to be aware of the importance of a healthy mind.

It is easy for the mind to run riot with fears and all manner of negative thoughts. This causes stress which adversely affects the organs of the physical body.

Taking control over thoughts isn't easy and requires much discipline but the rewards are great. Monitor your thoughts and you will find out how negative and destroying they can be. Be prepared to change your thoughts and you will find that positive thoughts lead to positive feelings which in turn benefit your physical body. Take several periods of relaxation and meditation each day and nourish your mind with affirmations.

It takes courage and trust to change your thinking, and also to believe that you are acting in your best interests. Take control of your thinking, drive out thoughts which damage your wellbeing, and you will achieve balance and health in body and mind.

In these modern times the rise of the gymnasium and health clubs has been swift. People have flocked to them to get their bodies into good shape. Some go to what seems like absurd lengths to do so, taking all sorts of supplements to "condition" their bodies.

We all eat, some better than others. By that I mean some have better diets than others. However we are all trying to nourish our bodies. We are trying to ensure that our bodies get the best possible fuel to keep us going about our daily business.

Do we ever nourish our minds? It is our minds that produce the thoughts that become ideas which in turn become our reality. And what do we feed it on? Mind numbing nonsense or thought provoking material? Do you really encourage your mind to exercise or do you just feed it low level stuff to keep it quiet?

Ask yourself what would become of your body if you treated it in the same way you treat your mind? How long would your body hold up on a low level diet of blandness?

Every one of us has a duty to exercise our minds, to look after them properly. Yes, we all have different levels of intellectual capacity and ability, but that shouldn't stop us from trying to nourish our minds.

When was the last time you examined your mind? Was it underachieving? Had it been bored rigid? What are you feeding your mind on? Like your body it needs the right nourishment, it needs to be stretched and exercised. You'll be amazed how much you know and how much you can achieve if you'd only nourish your mind.

When was the last time you examined your mind?

How often do you read inspirational books, or watch inspirational films?
How many hours do you devote to watching television?
What kind of programmes do you watch?
How beneficial is this?

The next time you are aware of fearful thoughts consider the detrimental effects of stress on your physical body.

Have you considered using positive affirmations in your quiet times?

31. When one door shuts look for one that is open.

It can be devastating when something you have enjoyed and which felt right for you comes to an end. There is often anger and hurt, plus a tendency to blame others for causing pain. It is easy to get into a rut and no effort is made to bring about change and progress.

Look for the benefits in these situations and grasp the opportunities which can open up. See this as your Higher Self working for you, encouraging you to journey in the right direction. Do not fight back at a physical level, clutching at straws which offer no support. Let go and look on the bright side knowing that other avenues are opening up.

Ask for guidance in your meditations and welcome the opportunities that arise. Do not be afraid of change. Do not have regrets either as everything in the past has had importance although it may have run its course. It has led you to where you are now. Have faith that there is a Divine purpose in everything and be grateful for the intervention of your Higher Self.

This is figurative. Doors closing is a symbol that there is no passage, either entry or exit. In most circumstances we will feel safe behind a closed door.

An open door is most always seen as an invitation. A chance to satisfy curiosity and take a look through it. Sometimes it is seen as the start of a new beginning, a fresh opportunity.

It is said that as one door closes another opens. It is almost as if you are being told which pathway to choose. When the door figuratively closes on you, either to prevent your entry or exit, you should ask why it has happened.

When you have discovered the reasons you will be in a better position to determine which of the open doors, (and there will be many), you should seek to enter. Ask yourself what each door will open for you. Consult your Inner Being. Life is a series of choices and this is why the greatest gift you have is free will. Free will is something that should never be given away, for you give away your whole being.

Choices are for you to make. Choices take courage to make. The open doors are all gateways -- which one will you choose?

Do not be afraid of change.

Take a look over your life at the incidents and events. Can you see that they are all connected in some way, that as one chapter closed a new chapter opened?

When faced with change do you react with fear or do you believe that the Universe is bringing you new opportunities?

Do you become upset when something you have enjoyed comes to an end?
Does focussing on what "has been" prevent you from seeing the benefits than "can be"?
Sometimes we need that push to move us on and upwards. Look for the pointers the Universe is giving you.

32. You cannot buy peace but you can create it.

No amount of money can guarantee peace or indeed other spiritual qualities such as love or joy. Money is a physical element created by man to satisfy physical needs. Indeed many rich people do not have peace or even good health in their lives. Qualities such as peace cannot be manufactured by one person and sold to another.

Peace is something you feel deep within your Being and no matter what turmoil is around you, it is still possible to be at peace within yourself.

Take time each day to be still and go within. The more often you do this the easier it becomes to find stillness and peace. Trust, and accept that there is a reason for everything and that you are being protected. The Universal plan is always right for you, and your Higher Self will ensure you are able to cope with any situation.

You can control your thoughts and hence your emotions. Choose to be peaceful and with that state of mind you are better able to confront whatever circumstances arise.

If at any time you feel ill at ease or disturbed take a few moments to go within to reconnect with your Higher Self. Bring this peace back with you, see the difference it can make and thank the Universe for making it freely available.

How many times have you heard or used the expression "Give me peace"? In all actuality peace is not a gift or commodity you can bestow on someone. Neither can you buy peace. Peace comes from within. It is a state of self comfort. True peace is born out of love, responsibility and a desire to maintain it. You cannot broker peace between individuals, groups or nations if they don't have it in their heart and are not committed to it. You can ease the tensions, you can pave a way, but you can't deliver unless everyone concerned wants it.

Peace begins with the individual. Inner peace occurs when you are doing the things you want to do, so long as this is not at the expense of others. When you are happy and content with your life you will discover Inner Peace, because that is what you will have created by your actions. As you do so, you will be an example to others, and so it grows. The domino effect. As you find peace you will be helping others to do the same.

When we all stop struggling and fighting, trying to ensure our will prevails, peace will spontaneously break out. We all have a responsibility to respect others for what they are -- sentient, spiritual beings. There will be those who have lost the connection and we who have retained or re-established it can help them to find theirs.

We need to change our thinking patterns so that we are giving out the right messages. When we think ill we get ill. When we give out fear and guilt we get the same back. Find peace within your heart then give it out. Peace will return in abundance. Take away the fear in your life and watch as the love and light flow in.

If you trust in the Universe you find that the Universe takes care of you. It is only because of your negative thoughts that you believe the Universe to be a dangerous place. If you change your thoughts you will find a Universe of Peace. How inspiring is that?

Choose to be peaceful.

How committed are you to finding peace?
How can you show this?

How much responsibility do you believe you can take for your feelings?
If you changed thoughts and beliefs would you find more peace in your life?

Do you ever blame others when you feel ill at ease?

33. The best healer you need is yourself

It is all too easy to give away your power to others, having high expectations of what they can achieve for you and trusting that they have the ability to do what you think you cannot do for yourself. There are many who can assist you when you are sick or go through difficult times, but ultimately all healing comes from within you.

How can others always know what is best for you. Acknowledge your own power, use it instead of not accepting responsibility and then blaming others when things go wrong.

Take time to make contact with your Higher Self. Ask for guidance and also for an understanding of what you have to learn from your experiences. Only your Higher Self understands why such and such a situation or illness has occurred, and what the reasons are for it.

Trust that you have the power to deal with whatever you have to face. Look after your physical body – only you can do this for yourself. Others may be able to advise you, but you are the one that has to act. Check out all advice with your Higher Self, then face up with courage to your responsibilities.

In your meditations send light and love to all your troubles. Do what you can to the best of your ability and ask the Universe to work things out in whatever way is right. The end result may not be what you expected but it will be the right answer. Quick fix healings are not always the best answer. Sometimes difficulties can take a while to work through and for lessons to be learned.

Only you know what is right for you but you have to link up to the Higher Realms for answers.

Do not give away your power but use your power wisely for lasting benefits.

Every difficulty you surmount will bring new understandings and you will learn to welcome situations instead of complaining. You cannot learn or achieve much if others take away your lessons from you. Say thanks for whatever comes your way, ask for guidance and be prepared to follow it through.

The world has many gifted individuals in medical practice who can do so much to alleviate pain and suffering. There are, too, countless others offering their skills in Spiritual and Energy Healing which bring relief to many. However the best healer we can use is ourself.

Traumas and illnesses are only outward manifestations of inner problems. We all carry baggage with us from our daily encounters with others with whom we come into contact. As we interact we can leave ourselves open to all sorts of psychological hurts. We can misinterpret others' words and actions. We can be aggressive or defensive. We form judgments and we let our judgments take root in our psyche.

We rarely try to resolve perceived problems as they occur, often preferring to take the line of least resistance, and we bury the problem further into our psyche.

It doesn't go away. It sits there unresolved and very often it grows inside like a tumour until it erupts into the physical as an illness or other trauma. Even although the problem has reached a critical stage we still do not resolve it properly. Yes, medical assistance can help. Yes, more subtle forms of healing can help. But the problem will not go away if we do not deal with it on a personal level.

This is where self healing is important, because if you do not or cannot resolve the basic issues then problems will persist.

You may feel you need help to face what lies at the root of your illness, that is understandable. The key to your self healing is taking personal responsibility for whatever has caused your suffering.

Every incident that occurs does so for a reason – this is how the Universe works. Every time you interact with another there is a lesson or message for both parties. If there is upset in the interaction do not react adversely but look for the message or lesson. Seek the positive from what appears to be a negative situation.

Be slow to anger and always keep an open mind. You can never make a judgment unless you know every fact. Do not hang on to anger, upset or grudge for you will never make progress. You have to settle your problem quickly and with love, then move on. Lighten your load. No other person can do this for you.

By letting go and sending love you heal yourself and also send positive feelings out to the Universe. Take responsibility, heal your situation, heal the world, heal the Universe.

Ultimately all healing comes from within you.

What could you do to take more responsibility for your health and wellbeing?

Do you believe that by putting trust in the Universe and letting go of fear your health would improve?

How well do you know yourself?
What steps could you take to get to know yourself better?

34. Self judgment brings forth purer intentions

There will often be times when you wonder if you are doing the right thing. You drift from one view to the other trying to convince yourself that what you are doing is for the best. When you judge others it's easy to convince yourself you are right and they have failed in some way.

Take time away from the situation and in these quiet moments reflect on what has been going on, and what part you have played. Did you become upset, critical, fearful, judgmental and rush in with decisions and actions which were not loving and which, perhaps, caused upset to others and rifts in relationships?

The most important thing to do is to look at your intentions. Were you out to get your own back on someone, were you jealous, faultfinding or even out to prove your own superiority?

How much love, unconditional love, was there in your intentions? Look carefully at your thoughts and actions as if you were an impartial outsider. If you are satisfied you were applying the Spiritual Laws, great, but, if not, some remedial action may have to be taken. If you feel something has to be said to another party do it lovingly to clear the air.

Be patient and understanding, not expecting them to have the same standards as yourself. Accept others as they are: set your boundaries with love. Change your intentions if they do not measure up to the loving standards you really do wish to maintain.

If your intentions are right your words and actions that follow will be right. Remember to look for the Angel in every person and that will allow you to operate from a spiritual perspective.

You are often quick to judge others, a trait we hope you are learning to curb. As we said before, you cannot judge another if you do not fully know them. There is always more to someone than meets the eye: the seemingly stern may have a soft side, the innocent looking may harbour a dark secret.

This leads us to ask "can you judge yourself?". Certainly you can, but the same restrictions apply: you have to know yourself first. How well do you know yourself? Have you ever sat yourself down and asked that question?

Consider your lifestyle, does it make you happy at the end of the day or do you get angry and frustrated pursuing a dream that is beyond your reach? Consider your beliefs, are they really yours or have they been placed upon your shoulders by others?

To really know yourself you have to ask deep questions about every aspect of your life. Not only that, but you need to come up with honest answers. There is no good trying to fool yourself, for it does you no good. You may fool others but you really can't fool yourself.

You need to shut yourself off from the physical world with all its attractions and distractions every now and again, and make serious contact with your Inner Self. Ask your Inner Self the difficult questions and listen carefully to the answers.

A combination of these two things will lead you into opening up your mind and considering what it is you are doing that makes you unhappy. It will lead you to what (or who) causes your anger and frustration. It will lead you back to the path you know you really want to be treading.

Doing all this leads you to knowing who you are and what it is you came to this lifetime to achieve. When you know who you are you can sit in true self judgment and from there you can fine tune your intentions so that you will reach spiritual enlightenment. Perhaps you can keep a journal of your daily activities, logging what it is you do and how you really feel.

How well do you know yourself?

What are you learning about yourself from your journal?
Is it helping you adopt more spiritual qualities?

How honest are you with yourself?

35. Conserve energy -- don't waste it in negative directions

Some people find it hard to comprehend, but the fact is everything in the physical world as well as in the spiritual world is composed of energy. Nearly everyone is aware that their energy levels fluctuate, and understand that they need sleep, healthy food and exercise to have energy to cope with day to day activities. Periods of rest and relaxation are important to allow the body to recuperate. However many fail to understand the need to take care of the mind as well as the body and that a healthy mind contributes much to physical wellbeing.

If there are anxieties preying on the mind these are continually churned around and the stress of the mind results in a stressed body, leading to ill health if this is not dealt with. Anxious thoughts, like all thoughts, are energy but they are wasted energy as there is usually no positive outcome.

With a positive disposition and pure loving thoughts filling the mind, it is easy to find answers to obstacles which beset us. Guidance can be received without blocking it out. When answers can be had from the Spiritual Self we are able to calm the mind and benefit from relaxation of both mind and body.

A racing mind uses up fuel like a racing car. Be like the still pond of clear water: unruffled, calm, reflecting peace to all around.

We are all energy and everything we think, do or say uses energy. We convert energy from one form into another, for instance from a thought to an action.

In other aspects of our life we use energy every day. We have utility companies who "generate" energy for our use to drive the wheels of industry and so forth. Without energy nothing would happen.

Energy is neither created nor destroyed. It merely changes form. The conversion process can be costly in whatever terms you want to apply – time, finance, danger. For this reason we all seem to be agreed that we should not waste what is available. But this agreement is like a physical response. We talk about insulating houses etc so that it takes less energy to heat them. We are treating energy here as a physical commodity and put a monetary value on it.

Seldom do we consider the spiritual side of energy, but we can apply the same precautions to it as we do to the physical product.

We turn thoughts into actions so it is in our best interests to make sure that they are for the common good. We send out negative mental responses to lots of situations. We hold grudges, we hang on to past indiscretions, we make snap judgments. Sometimes we do it just because we can. It is all wasted energy in that we could have used it for a positive purpose like sending out light and love, or giving praise or expressing joy.

What you give out you get back. Bad energy out means bad energy in and that leads to unhappiness, disappointment and even depression. On the other hand good energy out brings good energy in return with its associated feelings of happiness, elation and satisfaction. Keep your energy positive for maximum benefit.

A healthy mind contributes much to physical wellbeing.

Where does your energy go?
What do you expend it on?
How can you conserve your energy for positive activities?

How does stress affect your physical body and how do you normally cope with stress?
Could spiritual approaches provide more lasting benefits than your current coping mechanisms?

36. Do your best then ask the Universe to do the rest

You are part of the Universe and everything will work out best when you work as a team. It is important that you understand and use your own inner power, realising your potential to create your reality.

Whatever you are faced with, do whatever you can with love to sort things out in the best way for all involved.

There will always be circumstances over which you have no control. You cannot change others and it is wrong to try to control other people. They, like you, have free choice. From time to time you will experience circumstances which make you feel you are up against a brick wall.

When you feel you have done your best it is time to hand things over to the Universe and ask for help. Remember you are part of the Universe and the Universe knows your needs. You have to ask for help, and if you trust then things will work out in the right way.

Ask for help but do not become attached to a particular outcome. Be detached from a solution after asking for help or guidance. The Universe knows what experiences you need and what lessons you require to develop on your pathway.

Things will take their course and may end up differently from what you expected. Be patient and trusting at all times.

When you release your concerns and worries to the Universe you will feel much more relaxed. It will be like a weight off your shoulders. Continue to link up waiting for guidance as you will still have to play your part.

When you rely on the Universe to assist you, you will be amazed at how situations, which seemed insurmountable, can be resolved.

Work in partnership with the Universe and not in isolation.

When you set out to do something, anything, do it with the intention of doing the best you can. It's no good being reticent or half-hearted for this sends out entirely the wrong message to the Universe.

As you know, what you give out you get back. What goes round comes round. So if you are not giving it your best shot why should anyone else: why should the Universe? The Universe will take your sentiments, whatever they may be, positive or negative, and magnify them. Thus in some way this will return to you.

When you have put light and love into all that you do, the Universe will multiply it and move it around. If everyone did whatever they had to do with light and love imagine how wonderful everything would be and how exhilarated we would all feel.

Your self satisfaction would generate the same for others: theirs will generate more for you. When something needs doing do it to the best of your ability. If you do everything with this intention then the Universe will amplify your effort. Everyone will be better off spiritually, everyone will grow spiritually.

The Universe looks after our needs, that certainly is true. However the Universe gives back to us what we give out, so always do your best, do it with love and light and everyone will benefit in some way.

Work in partnership with the Universe and not in isolation.

What tasks, situations, relationships are you involved in that could do with some help from the Universe? Are you prepared to ask for this help and work with whatever answer you receive?

When you feel helpless try asking the Universe to sort things out but realise that you have to play your part.

37. Learn from the past but don't keep reliving it

Everything that confronts us has a purpose but we don't always look for the lesson we need to learn. Very often we get stuck in the past, going over events in our minds with anger, resentment and remorse. Sometimes we are unable to forgive and at other times we are filled with guilt and regret, wishing we could reclaim the past and relive it in a different way.

When we focus backwards into the past and channelling energy into what cannot be changed we are unable to be fully involved in the present. We are unable to concentrate on what we need to do now, and this means we do not function to the best of our ability in the present.

If you find yourself constantly going over what happened in the past look for the lessons to be learned so that mistakes are not repeated. Find it in your heart to forgive, even if others refuse to forgive you. Make it known to them if possible, but, if not, send out loving and forgiving thoughts to release you both from a negative past. It can only cause you and others harm to hold on to negative issues from past times.

If you feel guilty about something wrong you did or failed to do then do your best to forgive yourself. You can't change things now but you can let go and move on. The important factor is to learn from the past and move into the present with far greater wisdom and understanding. Learn, let go and move on with a determination to live as best as you can so that in the future you will have no regrets about the Now.

The longer you harbour grief about the past the harder it is to deal with it positively. At the end of each day take a few moments to go back over the day's events and look at what you needed to learn. Deal with any issues as quickly as possible so that you are free from any burdens which may weigh you down in the future. Learn from the present and the past will take care of itself.

Every event that occurs, every incident that you are involved in bears a message or a lesson. Nothing that happens does so for any other reason than to bring a message or offer a lesson.

In order to make spiritual progress you need to learn the lesson or understand the message. The Universe wants to help you develop on your chosen pathway so it will repeat the message or lesson until you learn.

That's why it sometimes seems as if you are in a rut, unable to climb out and get on with your life. The walls are too steep because you have missed the point. When you understand the message the sides of the rut will disappear and you can move on. Do certain things stick in your memory of incidents that have happened and you don't understand why? Are there relationships in your life that are uneasy or volatile? Why was someone else chosen for a position rather than you?

These sorts of questions can help you uncover messages from the Universe. Answering them honestly may help you understand what the Universe is trying to say to you. Ask your Higher Self for help in providing answers too. Your Higher Self knows your real agenda, and can offer assistance if you are deviating from it.

In going over events and incidents from the past remember that you cannot change them. You can only take out of them the message for yourself. When you have taken the answers on board you can change and get back to your life plan.

You do not have to relive the incidents and suffer all the negativity a second time. Merely go through the mechanics of what happened with light and love, and look for what the incident was trying to tell you. Do this in conjunction with your Higher Self and you will be astounded at the insights you gain. Then when you make adjustments to your self you will gain in confidence and happiness knowing that you are headed in the right direction and your destination is known.

> **Every event that occurs, every incident that you are involved in bears a message or a lesson.**

> In reviewing your journal what lessons have you learned from past events?
> Are you taking these on board?

38. Listen to others' points of view but remember you don't have to accept them as your own

It is good to be a patient listener especially when others have worries they wish to offload. It is also beneficial to hear what points of view others hold as this can be a way of gaining more knowledge. However, it is important to be discriminating as many people do their best to impose their views on others and they can be very forceful and dogmatic.

Listen to what is said but scrutinise others' views before adopting them as your own. Very often people go through life with very fixed beliefs which they have picked up in childhood from parents and teachers. These people are often well meaning and truly believe their views are the only correct ones so they do their utmost to instil them in others.

Once these beliefs are in the mind they can be hard to eradicate. Even in adulthood we are constantly faced with the opinions of other people everywhere we go, especially in the media. It is good to have an awareness of what others think and believe, but be sure to test these views against your own criteria before adopting them.

The best way to check out what you hear from others is to do so in your meditations. Get in touch with your Inner Self and ask if what you have heard is true for you. Everyone has a different view of truth and even individuals change their minds as they go through life in respect of what is true for them.

As you develop spiritually your views and ideas may change as you gain more wisdom. Therefore be willing to share with others what you believe but do not be dogmatic as you may change your beliefs in the future. Be tolerant of others at all times but remember that at any given time the truth for you is what you gain from within yourself.

In forming your beliefs and opinions it can be helpful to consult as wide a variety of counsel as possible. That way you can see all the arguments, hear all the facts. From such a wide panorama you can then form your own conclusions. When you have the wide picture before you, you can see all the aspects.

You can ask others for their views and opinions, still others will offer you their take on the matter, and still more will try to impose their view on you. Whatever opinions or beliefs others have are for them: they will use these to define who they are and what they are trying to achieve. That is, others' views fit their needs at any given time. Therefore, when others express themselves to you, listen, and listen carefully. Take note of what they say, for there will be pearls of wisdom in amongst all the counsel you receive: likewise, some expressions will cause you disdain.

When you have gathered all these differing ideas, thoughts, beliefs, opinions together you then have the task of sorting it all out. You need to keep hold of what resonates with you, and reject what feels not right for you at the time. Your Inner Self will help in this. Your Inner Self knows what your spiritual mission, your life plan, is and so will be able to give you intuition as to what fits with your goals.

Forming views, opinions, beliefs in this way will keep you on your chosen pathway and give you room to develop in a balanced manner. There will be no imposition by your Inner Self, only indications of what fits and seems best for you. You have the free will to make the choice.

Similarly, you should not feel that because you have asked another for their view, that theirs is the only way or even correct. If you don't agree you can politely say so and thank them for their help. If you truly want a set of beliefs to hang on to you need to form your own. Consult whosoever you want, but the final choice is yours, because to do otherwise is to step off your spiritual pathway.

You have the free will to make the choice.

Do you ever examine what beliefs and opinions you hold and wonder where they came from?
Are they truly yours or has someone else placed them there?

How difficult or easy do you find it to change your beliefs?

39. Never waste time – you cannot reclaim it

It is easy to meander through life without achieving much. Some live in the past going over misfortunes with regrets and others dream about the future, but take no positive action to achieve goals.

We have advised before to make the most of the present. Concentrate on what you can achieve now. Take positive steps each day to achieve whatever goals you have set yourself. When today has gone the time you had available for positive action will have gone with it.

Remember everyone incarnated on earth with a life purpose. Connect each day with your Inner Self and check that what you are doing is in tune with what you planned for your life path.

Even if, for some reason, you are unable to be physically active you can use time effectively with your thoughts. Send out love and healing thoughts to the sick, and also to the planet earth. Your thoughts are just as important as physical activities.

Negative thoughts and actions are wasted energy and wasted time. Take control of your life, be focussed on your spiritual journey. You will then be at peace with yourself with no regrets about what you could have done if you had constantly reminded yourself that time does not stand still.

You need to always live in the moment and for the moment, because if you don't you have lost it for ever. The moment is here and then it is gone, replaced by the next moment. Take what you can from the moment, do your best in the moment and all will be well. You will have no bad memories to worry over or anchor yourself to, and you can look back with happiness, knowing everything went well for you and others connected to you.

Too many people are trying to atone for past moments, lost moments, wasted moments and all they are succeeding in doing is wasting even more moments worrying about what they can never change.

If you have such worries then, please, let them go. Send light and love to them, send forgiveness if that is required, then release them. Reclaim your life by releasing the past with love.

Similarly you cannot anticipate the future otherwise you may miss out on the present. When you get there you will look back and worry about the time you wasted.

Now is where you are and now is where your focus is best centred. Sure, look back at the past and bring forward the learning that occurred. Sure, plan for the future but be prepared to be flexible and willing to change plans as events develop between now and then, and they will.

The Universe is bountiful, the Universe is abundant. See the truth in this and you will realise that your needs are always met. Even in your darkest night the Universe shines a light to guide you.

Worrying about the past or the future is for time wasters. You can do nothing about changing either. You can influence the latter but only if you concentrate on the present moment. You have to do it this way or you have wasted an opportunity.

Your thoughts are just as important as physical activities.

Examine where your time goes over a three day period by keeping a record of everything you do and how long each item / activity takes.

Where can you make improvements?
How much time is spent on self-development?
Do periods of quiet receive priority?

How focussed are you on what you seek to achieve?

40. See with your Soul and notice how better the view is

Your physical eyes have a very narrow, limited view. Sight is very important for getting through physical activities on the earth plane. However, if you are aware that you are a spiritual being seeking to progress at a higher level then you will realise how important it is not to just accept everything at face value. If you allow yourself to function only at a material level your Ego will step in and influence your thinking about what you see.

Whatever is in view, always take time to check it out at a spiritual level. Your Soul has the overall picture and knows how all the pieces fit together. Judging is what you are tempted to do at a physical level but wisdom and understanding come into place at Soul level.

Your Soul knows what is right for you and understands the linking of events and the opportunities for development.

If you trust your Soul and ask for the strength and support to get through whatever comes to you, you will not grumble about events and judge others harshly as you will have insight as to why certain things occur and even as to how they link up with each other.

There is a purpose behind all things which is not often evident at first sight. Close your eyes and ask your Soul to direct and guide you. Ask your Soul to illuminate your path and be willing to trust that your Soul knows best.

Your Soul will allow you to see the positive in everything and everyone, giving you a wider and deeper perspective at all times.

When you look around you what you see gets processed by your physical body. When you look at a landscape, a view, you convert what you see through your filters into meaningful images. Then you place a judgment on it. You compare it to other places you have been. You compare it, perhaps, to preconceived ideas you have generated from photographs or other people's descriptions.

You may marvel at what you see or you may condemn it – you have judged the physical by the physical, and, depending on your verdict, you will generate an emotional response. For instance you may feel disappointed or you may enthuse about it.

You do this when you meet other people too. You process them through your physical mechanisms and make judgments about them without really knowing them. You sum them up by their and your physical attributes. You are more often than not guided by your Ego in doing so. People are usually categorised by how useful they are to your Ego's purpose.

What if you looked at everything in a different way? Would it make a difference? Would you still reach the same end result?

Try looking at everything from the Soul's point of view. Look for the spiritual with your Spiritual Being. See how the view changes. You will see the inherent beauty in nature. You will truly marvel at what the Universe has created. If you take yourself off to a quiet location and sit there in inner contemplation you will discover a new world.

You will hear the sounds of the Universe – the birds singing, the water rippling, the waves crashing, the wind as it moves through the trees and over the land. You will discover Nature in all its beauty and glory. It truly is a magnificent feeling. When you let time just disappear, and commune with Nature your Spiritual Being will grow far beyond the confines of your physical body.

When you have done this and experienced the glory you will want to look at other people in the same way. You will see them for what they are – Spiritual Beings like yourself. You will see all their positive aspects. You will see them as you never have before. When you do this you encourage others to do it too. When we all view this world with our Soul we will truly have found paradise.

Like all journeys, the journey to paradise starts with a small step. Be a leader and take that step. Open up your Soul and see a better world.

Look for the spiritual with your Spiritual Being.

Where, in nature, would you like to be right now?
You can go there by sitting in the quiet and visualising
it. Try it and see how refreshed you feel afterwards.

What prevents you from seeing the Divine in others?
How can you become more aware of others' spiritual
qualities?

Are you quick to make judgments or do you take a
spiritual approach trusting there is good in everything
and everyone?

41. Spring clean your mind to clear away the debris

Many of you carry much in your minds which you could do better without. From childhood, right through adulthood you are subjected to ideas, thoughts, remarks and beliefs which come from others and very often these are unpleasant and negative. They are absorbed by your unconscious mind and you come to believe they are correct.

Take time to get to know the real you and not what others would have you believe. Examine why you do certain things in particular ways, examine your beliefs about both yourself and the outside world. Are you being true to yourself? Are you open to communication with your Higher Self and doing your best to follow the guidance which comes from your Higher Self?

In order to follow your spiritual pathway you need to clear out beliefs from your mind which do not fit in with your Higher ideals. Be yourself. It takes courage to change, courage to change your ways and ideas which have been part of you for a long time.

Free yourself from the chains of the past, check out with your Inner Self what comes to you from others. If it doesn't feel right let it go. Keep an open mind at all times. Let in what's right and dispense with what you would class as clutter. Use your inner strength to control your mind. Allow your mind to work for you and not against you.

Your brain is more powerful than any computer that man can devise. It does so many things automatically that it never stops being active during your physical life. It's in the brain that ideas are formed and information stored. It's in the brain that your beliefs are formed and held, and where judgments are made and remembered.

Everything that you do comes from the brain, everything that happens to you is remembered by the brain.

The mind, whilst perhaps not a physical entity as such resides in the brain and can be regarded as the brain's controller.

Sometimes we have so much in our mind / brain that everything gets cluttered and we do not function as well as we could. Sometimes we hold on to too many things like grievances and missed opportunities that we appear to run out of room for newer thinking. Thus we get stuck in the past and can't move forward.

From time to time we need to sit down with ourself and take a look at what's going on. We need to examine how we are utilising this great resource we have. Is it functioning at its best or could it be improved?

Are we hanging on to things from the past that use up energy negatively? Can we take some items and discard them, with love and light, to free up resources for new ventures?

In our physical lives we have clearouts on a regular basis in order to give ourselves room in which to live, so why not take the process a step further and clear out the mind of items, thoughts, beliefs, judgments, etc we no longer need? This would leave us more open minded and better prepared and able to take on new ideas, beliefs, etc. So take some time to sit in the quiet and consult with your Higher Self to see what can safely be discarded.

Allow your mind to work for you and not against you.

What's on your mind at this moment that may be holding back your spiritual development?

Are you willing to change your beliefs as you develop or is it more comfortable to keep the beliefs you've always had?

42. The lighter your load, the faster you travel

You can move faster in a physical sense when you have only a light load to carry. Heavy items weigh you down and progress is slow and tiresome. The journey can be painful as well since you are putting stress on your body.

The same is true at a spiritual level. If you seek to progress well on your spiritual life path then it is necessary to dispense with whatever would slow you down.

Take stock of what you carry in your mind and what negative emotions have built up from past events and relationships. If you are holding on to fear, grudges, disappointments, anxieties, guilt, then these are what will occupy your thought process. These will weigh you down causing a lowering of mood and even depression.

Learn from what has gone before but be willing to let go of what hinders your progress. Bring in the light to shine on these events and on those who have been part of your unpleasant experiences, asking for a blessing on all.

As your emotions lighten and you allow light to flow through your entire being you will begin to see clearly why difficulties occur and appreciate the lessons they present.

You will learn to trust, you will have a new understanding of why you came into this incarnation and you will realise that every problem can be overcome with unconditional love.

Divine light will lighten your load and you will have nothing to halt your progress.

When you have a load to carry it affects the speed at which you can travel. If your load is too heavy then you may not be able to move at all.

However, these words are not aimed at the physical side of your life, although many parallels can be drawn therefrom. These words are aimed at the mental, emotional and spiritual sides of your being. You could almost say they are directed at your psychological baggage.

Is your life heavy laden with problems, worries, grudges, anger, resentments? Do you look back at past events with regret? Do you have vengeance on your mind? These are all examples of heavy baggage, a load that will stop you in your tracks. These are the kinds of things that will anchor you in the past, tethered like some poor animal unable to get to where you really want to be, to where you know you should be.

Is your life full of "if only …."? This holds you back too because it leads to regret, anger and self deprecation.

If your life is like this then a change is long overdue. You need to jettison some or all of this baggage. Look at situations that are pulling you backwards, send love and light to them, then let them go. Let the light of the Universe shine into your darkness. Yes, lighten up! Lighten your load and see how you move forward on your spiritual pathway. When you have the light on your way ahead your load will always be bearable.

Take time to go into the quiet, and in your meditation consult with your Inner Self. Bring in the light until there are no shadows, for if there are no shadows there is no hiding place for negative thoughts.

When your very Being is filled with light what joy you will encounter. When you are filled with light you will know you are living out your life plan. When you are filled with light you will be a beacon of positive energy shining for all to see.

What you give out you get back, the Universe will see to that. Positive brings positive, light brings light. Moving forwards means you will reach the goals you set for yourself. There is no need to weigh yourself down with energy sapping negativity.

Shine your light for all to see and move forwards confidently and positively.

Is your life heavy laden with problems, worries, grudges, anger, resentments?

How do you deal with problems?
Do you face up to them or do you ignore them hoping they'll go away of their own accord?

What negativity are you carrying with you which could be released by unconditional love and forgiveness?

Have you considered how much stress your physical body suffers because of negativity in your mind?
Is it worth it?

Think back to a time when a weight was suddenly lifted from your mind and remember how good it felt.
Would you like to feel like this more often?

43. If you shine like the stars you will be seen in the darkness

The stars are always there but the greater the darkness the greater their brightness. It is a wonderful feeling to view the brightness of the stars on a clear, cloudless night. The stars like everything in the Universe have a vital part to play and provide a guiding light to those who can identify them and know their location.

When you allow your inner light to shine, you can be a beacon for others. You have to rise above your own difficulties, learning from them and trusting that all your needs are met. This enables you to maintain love and joy in your heart which can be seen by others. When others go through what seems like a dark tunnel, where there is little hope of improvement they will be attracted to that shimmer of light and hope which radiate from you. They will gravitate towards you as they will have an inner sense that you can provide hope and upliftment.

What you learn from your own experiences will enable you to guide and assist others who walk in darkness, and seek your help. There is no need to force help on others as they will be guided towards your light at the right time.

Be a guiding light for others, leading them to their destination just like the bright stars in the sky.

When you bring forth light into your entire being you are not just a channel for your own benefit but you are serving many others as well.

Light is necessary for growth. Look how insects and plants rise up to the light. Be a point of growth for others and you will increase your own light at the same time.

Everyone is a spiritual being, everyone is a light ready to shine out. However, not enough of you allow your light to shine outwards. You keep it hidden, sometimes too afraid, for many reasons, to let it be seen. Never be afraid or ashamed to shine out. It shows you know who you are and are travelling on your spiritual path.

If everyone allowed their light to shine out you could dispel the darkness forever, but these times are some way off yet. However, those who can shine should do so. It is almost a condition of walking the pathway that you let your light shine. Not only will you see where you are going, others will see you too.

Shining your light is a comfort for others. Seeing that you are treading your path means they are not alone in treading theirs. When groups of people walking the spiritual path come together the light they send out is so much stronger and can be seen from further away. Thus you are sending out a message over a great distance.

It is like the stars: they shine in your darkness. They may seem like little spots of light, but you know that they are enormous and are sending their light over amazingly huge distances. On a clear, cloudless night you will see an uncountable number of stars in the sky. You can navigate by them, you can tell the time of year by them. Endlessly, they shine out and what a comfort they can be in an otherwise blackened situation.

Take the stars as a positive example and shine out. Let the world see who you are. Take solace from seeing all the other lights. No one is alone on their spiritual path. There is nothing to fear in the darkness, for there will be many lights shining through it.

Be a guiding light for others.

In what ways can you let your light shine?

How willing are you to assist others who need help?

How much better do you feel when you have helped others, even in some small way?

44. If you think you're a failure you've failed to think positively

When circumstances do not work out as you would like, or relationships become acrimonious, perhaps even crumbling, it can be all to easy to blame oneself. Perhaps you blame yourself for not doing enough or for doing too much. You may think you took the wrong action or even believe you failed because you remained inactive.

Take what is positive out of every situation and relationship. Whatever occurred did so for a reason. What you have to do is to analyse what occurred, the part you played, and to look for the spiritual lessons which will enable you to develop your spiritual qualities.

Do not become angry and upset with yourself or with others. Criticism and regret are qualities which will reinforce your belief that you have failed in some way. Dispense with negative self talk, look at what you have learned and put your positive aspects into action in the future.

It is also important to believe in yourself and dispense with negative views others have about you. It's what you believe about yourself that is important.

Learn to say thanks for everything that occurs. Know that you can use all situations to advance spiritually. Continually look to your Higher Self for guidance. Your Higher Self never sees you as a failure. You are a spiritual being with infinite potential but you have to believe this, otherwise you fail to progress. Believe in yourself, know that even if you could have done better there is always a next time to put what you have learned into practice.

It is better to know there is always room for improvement than to believe you are a failure or to believe you are always perfect. If you fail to understand how you can advance spiritually then your level of development will be stagnant.

There are times in everyone's life when they have given up when confronted with a situation. They may have tried many things to resolve it, indeed many can claim that they tried everything they knew to reach a satisfactory conclusion. Then they have turned away from it and gone off in a different direction.

Is that what you do when confronted by setbacks? Do you just throw up your hands in frustration and anger, and walk away never to return to the problem?

In reality the problem remains unsolved and all you have done is to shower the Universe with negativity. As you know, this will be returned to you, so every failure you have will, at some stage, come back to haunt you. What goes round comes round.

Every situation, every event, every problem has an answer: there is always an outcome. Sometimes the resolution is simple and quick, sometimes it is difficult and challenging. Walking away is not an answer, it is not a satisfactory conclusion. Only when both sides are happy with the outcome can you say it has been resolved.

When problems occur, they do so for a reason. There is a message for you. In challenging situations you will obviously have to devote more time to see the message: you will be tried in many ways and on many levels.

If you take the knowledge that there is always an answer into your problem solving, then you will be taking positivity into the process. See the situation as a challenge and be positive and confident about producing an answer.

Others involved will become more positive too and so the resolution will likely arrive sooner rather than later. However this is not to say that you may require to work hard and display skills during the process.

You can always call on your Higher Self to help you reach a satisfactory outcome. In your meditation or quiet time you can ask for help. The answer may not come immediately, but it will come.

If you have confidence in yourself this will be reflected back by the Universe. You will receive positive energy. The energy circulates: from you to the Universe, back to you, out to those you have dealings with, out to the Universe, back to individuals. The circulation is endless.

When you think positively you cannot fail, so take heart and know the answer is waiting.

Take what is positive out of every situation and relationship.

What prevents you from looking for the lessons from situations and relationships?
What steps do you need to take to be able to see the positive that is in every situation, event and relationship?

See mistakes as a learning opportunity and be thankful for them.

We all have talents and abilities: what are yours?
How can you put them to full use?

To what extent have others influenced you to believe that you were no good at something?
Was it a mistake to keep believing what you were told?

45. Tell the Universe your difficulties but let it decide how to deal with them

When faced with situations which cause hurt or fear many people turn to prayer for help. When you feel you've done everything you can, and you still feel upset, prayer can seem the only thing left to try. It is good to pray and ask for help, and indeed the Angels and your guides are always available to love and support you.

However, do not expect instant solutions as it is not in your best interests for the Universe to meet your every request, at least not in response to what you demand. You may think you know best but the Universe will sort things out in the right way for everyone.

Everything happens for a reason, and the reason may not always be immediately evident. You can't have an overview of everything at a physical level. Whatever happens, you have something to gain spiritually, but this may take time and a quick fix would gain you nothing. It may be you have to acquire more trust, patience, tolerance, or acceptance for example, and a quick solution would deny you the opportunity to grow.

Therefore we encourage you at all times to ask for help and guidance. Be silent so that you do not miss out on guidance being given.

Look back on your life at situations which were uncomfortable or even unpleasant. Take time to look at what positive qualities or learnings you gained from them and realise that it took time to gain benefit.

Trust the Universe to have your best interests in mind and your difficulties will be a blessing in disguise.

There are times when it seems as if all your troubles have landed on your shoulders at the same time and you are weighed down so heavily that you feel you cannot move. Indeed there are many people who, when this happens, just crumble, fall apart, totally defeated, demoralised and depressed.

In times like these it seems there is nowhere to go and no one to help you in your hour of greatest need. All the negativity flows through you and you sink even deeper, if this is possible, into self destruction.

No matter how hard you try, or how much you want to change things around, everything you do turns to stone. You are at a loss as to what to do next.

Everything is going wrong because your Ego is driving you: it is making decisions. It is Ego that is trying to extricate itself from the situation. Ego is selfish and will not come up with the required answer. Sometimes you can see the answer but Ego will not let you pursue it.

Know this: you are not alone and help is at hand. Your spiritual body is with you, your Higher Self. Your Higher Self never leaves you, never gives up on you. It is your companion and guide through this physical life you have chosen to live.

Through your Higher Self you are connected to the Universe, the Source, the Godhead – call it what you will. If you connect to your Higher Self and communicate with it, you are connected to All that there is – the Universe. All is One and One is All.

It is best to be always in touch with your Higher Self, checking out where you are in relation to your life plan. In times of great difficulty that connection can bring you back on track.

Tell the Universe what your problems are: tell the Universe that you would like to get back to your life plan. Ask for help to resolve your difficulties and get back on your chosen pathway. You may get an immediate response, but this isn't always the case. When you tell the Universe your difficulties you should detach yourself from them and allow the Universe to deal with them. The Universe will react in an appropriate fashion and something will be done when the timing is right for all concerned.

Trust that the Universe is working for you. Send light, love and positive feelings to your situation and to all involved in it. Send out these vibrations to the Universe and know that an answer is being worked out. As you give so shall you receive. What you give out you get back.

The Universe is working for you. After all you are part of it: we are all one. When you realise this then you know that One will not harm itself and when a part of the One is in pain then the rest will do what's necessary to heal that pain and bring the Whole back into balance.

Trust that the Universe is working for you.

What keep you attached to outcomes?

How can you put more trust in the Universe?

The Universe can take time to bring about the right solutions. Do you have the patience to wait for this?

46. You are the driver on your pathway. Don't blame others if you don't reach your destination

We have indicated many times how much power you have within yourself and how important it is to use this power positively to create your own destiny.

You incarnated with a life plan which your Higher Self knows and understands. Link up daily for guidance as to how you can achieve what you set out to do in this lifetime.

It is easy to become distracted from taking action to pursue what is right for you. Work, relationships, unforeseen events can make it difficult to stay on course. It can be an easy way out to blame others or circumstances over which you seem to have no control. It becomes more difficult to get back on track the longer you have deviated from it. It is good to show care and compassion when others need help but do not allow yourself to be manipulated or controlled.

Keep focussed on your destination whilst still being flexible when circumstances necessitate it.

Remember how powerful your thoughts are and how these shape your reality. Keep your goal in mind and in your quiet times reaffirm your commitment to achieving it. Ask for ideas and guidance and send out positive thoughts which will bring positive outcomes. Visualise what it will be like to reach your destination and surround it with love and light.

Do not become dismayed by setbacks or rebuffs from others. Remember there is a reason for everything and the learning experience will see you through the next stage of your journey.

Your pathway will not always be straight or simple. There will be detours to make and crossroads to negotiate. Stay in control with a loving attitude and you will be glad you took responsibility throughout your journey. Remember the other drivers on the road may seem awkward and difficult but they, in some way, will be assisting you on your life path.

The great thing about being who you are is that you know where you are going and how you are going to get there. You may have been, or may still be, distracted by the physical world and how it operates. You may have forgotten your commitment to your spiritual self, lost it in the lower vibrations of the earth plane.

But that is beside the point, for you are still responsible for getting to your destination and completing the tasks you set for yourself. It may be that you have to reincarnate, perhaps more than once, to get to that destination, but eventually you will reach it.

You can make efforts to get yourself on track by consulting your Inner Being. If you shove your Ego out of the way and give your Inner Being some attention you will again be heading in the right direction. When you made your commitment and set out your pathway your Inner Being took note of what these are.

Unlike your physical being which is dominated by Ego, your Inner Self remembers your ambitions, indeed it can never forget them. Neither can it give you false information when you ask it to provide answers to "who am I?" and "why am I here?" .

As a being you have free will to do as you choose, pick any pathway or lifestyle you like. You behave as you see fit, pick and choose your friends and so on. However this does not negate the absolute responsibility you have to achieve your spiritual goals. As stated earlier, the Universe will see that you carry out your side of the bargain, if not in this lifetime, then in another or another.

Because you have this innate responsibility to the Universe you cannot simply use the excuse that you forgot, or others pulled you from the pathway – they simply are not true.

You can always get in touch with the one true Source that knows of your mission by entering the quiet and making contact, preferably on a regular basis. That way you will know how well you are progressing against the criteria you set.

As for it being the fault of others, then sorry, that is also down to you. You have this wonderful gift of free will so do not misuse it to seek out the physical pleasures or to join activities that may drive you from your stated objectives.

You are a spiritual being in a physical body and are here to pursue your spiritual agenda. The physical world is a challenge you have to pass through. Your spiritual end is within you – you have to let it out. Instead choose not to suppress it for the life of the physical distractions.

Only one person can ensure you reach your spiritual goals. Only one person can oversee you achieving your spiritual objectives. Others can help or hinder, but only you can do it.

Only one person can ensure you reach your spiritual goals.

What are your spiritual goals?
What are you hoping to achieve in this lifetime?
How will you know when this has happened?

When you are using your talents and abilities in service to others you will be well on the way to achieving your life plan.

Are you willing to take responsibility for what occurs in your life?
Remember you get back what you give out. Realise your potential and take appropriate action to achieve your goals.

47. There is much to learn from nature but you need to take time to connect

Everything in the Universe is connected. You are part of nature and everything in nature is part of you. All is Source: All is One. If you recognise this connection you will be more fulfilled and balanced in your daily life.

Nature has much to teach us and spending time in nature is the best way to learn. This is especially important as it is all too easy to join the rat race with little time to unwind, or connect with your Higher Self, to enable you to direct your attention away from earthly tasks.

Time is precious, work takes priority and even finances take precedence over spiritual development.

Every day take time out to become at one with any natural experience. Sit against a tree, feel your bare feet on the grass, welcome the sunrise or absorb the beauty of a sunset. Feeding the birds, enjoying the sunshine or taking a walk during a refreshing shower of rain can give you time to appreciate what nature is about.

The birds find food without having to store it up and worry about the future. The seasons bring about the right amount of sun and rain to grow our food. The natural rhythm of nature, whether it is in day or night, winter or summer, allows everything to flourish at the right time. The animals and birds know when to work and when to rest. They do not push themselves beyond the limits and yet they survive.

Nature can show us how to find a natural rhythm in our lives, how to let go and trust that we will be taken care of.

It's all about time and trust and knowing that if it works for nature it will work for you. If you let go of the unnatural rhythms to which you often subject yourself, you will find peace and health, physically and spiritually.

Your lives are all about rushing here and there. You have places to be, people to see. There are deadlines to be met. Some of you never stop from early morning until late at night. Always active, always having several irons in the fire, juggling tasks, trying to please everyone.

Then you wonder where your life went. You didn't take time to live it, you let others set your agenda and you flitted here, there and everywhere trying to fulfil another's wish.

Ask yourself this "does nature get itself into such a panic as people do?" No, it certainly doesn't. Nature goes on at a pace that is convenient for the purpose. Nature doesn't set deadlines and doesn't rush from pillar to post. Nature does as Nature needs to do.

In nature there is a time and a place for everything. Always has been, always will be. Nature will still be here long after people have gone.

People can try to control Nature, but in the end Nature adapts and can't be controlled. Yes some species have become extinct because man has not understood the order of things and has hunted certain birds, animals and fish until there were none left.

Man has tried to change Nature with disastrous consequences too. When will man ever learn?

Have you ever taken yourself off to a secluded garden, park, coastal area, forest and just sat there, quietly, watching nature? Mother Nature is the most wonderful teacher you could ever have. She provides the right environments and conditions for all creatures, man included, who want to live. She adapts when things go wrong.

When have the birds not sung, or the flowers failed to bloom? Nature sees that these events happen, quietly, without fuss, at the right time. Nature adores life, nature encourages life, nature provides for life.

Where does your lifestyle fit in with nature? How does it fit in? Are you making any effort to live with nature? Do you make any positive contributions to nature? Maybe you are too wrapped up in your egocentric, physical world, trying too hard to keep up with the demanding pace and the unspiritual dogmas. Maybe you don't care about nature: that would be such a shame.

You are part of nature and not in confrontation with it. Nature has much to offer you in so many ways if you would only stop and take notice. If you succeed in killing off nature, your world will end, so stop and think about what you are doing and recognise there is a better way to live.

Where does your lifestyle fit in with nature?

Do your activities reflect the seasonal cycles?
Do you take time out to recover and regain your strength?

How frequently do you spend time in nature?

If you cannot go for walks in nature try surrounding yourself with plants, flowers or other natural items and notice the difference this makes.

Nature has her own natural rhythm. To what extent does stress affect the natural rhythm of your body?

48. Not everyone can see Angels but everyone can ask them for help

Angels are beautiful Beings of Light. They are known as "messengers of God" but only some people are able to see them. It doesn't matter whether or not you can see them with your physical eyes.

What is important to understand is that they are ever present and waiting for you to call out to them for help and guidance. They bring an infinite number of spiritual qualities such as love, peace, healing, joy, but will only assist if you request it. As with all spiritual help whether it is from Ascended Masters, Angels or Archangels, it will only be given upon request as all these Beings respect your free choice.

If you do not see Angels never doubt their presence. Call on them for whatever assistance you require and trust that they will respond. Whenever you have a problem share it with the Angels. It may be healing that you require, help with a relationship, or even everyday difficulties such as the need to locate a lost item or even to find a parking space. You can ask the Angels to fill your home with love and even to go with you each time you leave home.

Make friends with the Angels and work in partnership with them. You will never know how much help is available to you until you give the Angels a chance. Don't wait for a crisis to cry out to the Angels: start working with them now so that you can build up your trust in them. These unseen friends can uplift you in amazing ways.

Some of you are blessed with the talent, the ability to see Angels and other Beings of Light. A few of those who have this ability are not comfortable with it, for whatever reason: however, most of those who can see Angels realise what a wonderful gift they have been given. It's one thing to see Angels and another to know that they are there: therefore Angels are available to all, if only everyone would realise this.

Angels surround you. Everywhere you go, everything you do, Angels are with you. Everyone has a Guardian Angel, a special friend, comforter and guide to help you when you ask. Don't think you are ever truly alone because your Guardian Angel walks every step of the way with you, shares your good times and comforts you in your bad times.

It is usually in times of crisis or need that people call on the spiritual elements for help. When you send out a prayer or call for the Universal Spirit to help, that plea is heard by all the Angels, and they will do what they can to assist.

Angel help manifests in many ways from an actual appearance to very subtle acts. Angel answers are not always immediate and often people think that the Angels have neglected them, or worse still, don't exist. It is not true. Angels do exist and they will help. You just have to be patient and look for the signs.

In your quiet time or in your meditation send out love to the Angels and they will pass this round the Universe. Your love helps enlighten everyone. Similarly, others' love will help you when you need it.

In your quiet time you can make contact with your Guardian Angel, just as you contact your Higher Self. Whatever you ask your Higher Self you can ask your Guardian Angel. As you develop your contact you may become aware of other spiritual beings close to you. You can ask them for help too when you need it.

For those seeking to travel their spiritual path there are many willing helpers, you just have to call on them. Seen or unseen they will assist you in reaching your destination.

Whenever you have a problem share it with the Angels.

What could you ask the Angels to help you with today?
Remember to thank them for the help received.

Keep entries in your journal to remind you of ways in which the Angels have taken care of you.

49. It's not just friends who are special, enemies are too

Friends are important in our lives and it is to friends we often turn when there's a crisis. True friends are special in that they are there to share problems with us as well as to share pleasant times. It is when we have troubles that we find out who our friends really are. They are the ones who are willing to go the extra mile, or listen to us as we offload our concerns and worries.

Whilst we usually appreciate friends it is very often difficult to appreciate enemies. When we find others hurtful or difficult to get along with it would seem as if we could do better without such people in our lives. However, they play just as an important part as friends, although in a different way. Every person we meet, just like every event, is there for a reason.

These aren't chance encounters which we find a hindrance or which make us annoyed. These people play a vital part in our lives as they give us an opportunity to search for our own spiritual qualities. Sometimes we can show forgiveness, other times we can show unconditional love, patience and even learn to be non-judgmental and less critical. It is easy to see the God in friends but not so easy to see the Divine in those who do not like us.

If we can see past the problems our enemies present, and realise they too are spiritual beings giving us the opportunity to grow then we will understand that they are giving us a service for which we should be grateful.

In your quiet moments send out love to your enemies and you will be amazed at how situations can change for the better. Love your enemies as you do your friends for they are every bit as special.

You all like to have friends around you: they give you comfort, they give you support, they give you love. You pick your friends carefully, for these are the people who will become closest to you. Those whom you especially like will be very special people: people in whom you will confide any problems you may have.

Yes, friends are very special people. You will share your secrets with them, and they with you. You will reflect the glories of yourselves to each other. You become a cosy group, and often it is hard for others to break into your world because you have formed a clique and put up invisible boundaries.

Sometimes you give away part of yourself to the group and a communal identity takes over. Your actions are not really your own, but are those of the group. You think alike, you act alike, sometimes you even dress alike.

But don't you think that, cosy and comfortable this arrangement may seem, it is a dangerous liaison in some respects? You separate yourself from everyone else. You cut yourself off from true reality. You become predictable and stereotyped. You and your group can even become egocentric and conceited.

In all probability you will have become judgmental about others – how they live, what they think and so on.

But really if you have become as we have outlined above, then happy as you seem to be you have lost your way at a spiritual level. This is when your perceived enemies become just as special, or even more so, as your friends.

You need to be brought back to reality with a bump, and that's exactly what your enemies will do. They will tell you what you are doing wrong: in your thoughts, in your words and in your deeds.

It may hurt and dismay you to hear what is being said about you, but if you shove your Ego out of the way you will hear words of truth. Enemies are very good at bringing you back to the real world from your wanderings and that's what makes them so special.

If you would just take time to take a long hard look at yourself you would see that there is always room for improvement. Listening to your enemies more often will result in that improvement. Isn't that special?

Love your enemies as you do your friends for they are every bit as special.

How do you define your friends?
Do they protect you from reality?
Do they politely agree with you at every turn?

What positive qualities can you display when someone upsets you?

List three positive qualities for every person you find it difficult to get on with.

In your meditation send love and light to those you find difficulty getting on with and thank them for what they are teaching you.

50. Don't give up, link up

When someone says they "give up" they infer there is no hope of improvement to a situation or condition. Some give up straight away without making an effort as they feel all is lost. Others struggle and battle on but come to the conclusion that their efforts are wasted.

Sometimes these words come from other people telling someone with a problem that their struggle is fruitless.

When you find yourself in situations like this you can only do your best, and if others are involved then you cannot change their views by thinking you can control them.

Do whatever you can to resolve your difficulties. If there are obstacles over which you have no control then all you can do is to link up with your Higher Self and seek guidance.

Be sure to listen for ideas, symbols, words which may assist you. At times guidance may come days or even weeks after you have asked for help and may come in ways you never anticipated. You may suddenly meet someone who can assist, or be guided to a place or even read something which will be meaningful.

You may not be given any guidance regarding actions at all, as action at a physical level may be out of the question. Always ask for love, light and healing to go where it is needed. Hand over your difficulties to your Higher Self and Angels, and you will be surprised at what they can achieve for you. Don't give up but believe that everything is possible with love.

In all our channellings there has been a steady reference to this very subject. Largely our message has been, and continues to be, to make and keep contact with your Higher Self.

Hopefully we have explained that All is One: that everything is connected; that all of the Universe is one entity. We have brought you the message that everyone and everything in your physical world is part of the greater whole: without even one little part there can be no wholeness.

People try all sorts of measures, mostly born out of frustration, anger and desperation, when serious trouble pays them a visit. They somehow fix themselves in the physical, thinking that the physical is all there is.

It has been our intention to show you that there is far more than this, and that if you take your problems to a higher level, that is, the spiritual level, you can make breakthroughs you perhaps thought were not possible to achieve.

As we have said before, giving up doesn't solve anything. At some stage you have to return to face the problem you tried to walk away from. When you try to walk away, you will find you carry the reminders and memories in your psychological baggage and these can weigh heavily on you.

We have encouraged you, almost at every turn, to "go inside" and discover the real you: we will always advocate this course of action. It is through your Inner Being that you maintain your connection to the Universe, to the Source, to the Oneness. Everyone has this connection: a small number have their connection permanently switched on and in constant use; some make use of it occasionally whilst most are totally unaware that it exists.

Those who use their connection freely walk their spiritual path just as they planned to do: they know who they really are, what they are on this plane to do, and so know where they are going. They also let their inner light shine to inspire others to make the connection. They are willing helpers for those trying to switch on.

Those who use the connection on occasions generally do so only when things start to get tough. It's almost a last desperate bid to solve their trouble. When all else fails say a prayer. As soon as the Universe responds positively they revert to their physical lifestyle until the next crisis. These people are not hearing the message, not learning the lesson, so the message will be repeated until they do learn.

The vast majority who are totally switched off are, if you like, living in the fast lane. They take risks, they play hard and fast with no thought of consequences. They dismiss the spiritual as having no truth or basis. They are completely earthbound. They will remain so, for many lifetimes in some cases, until they literally see the light.

You came to this plane in this lifetime with a definite spiritual plan, goals to achieve, enlightenment to find. For most, the distraction of physical life has caused amnesia of that life plan. You can get back on track when you switch on your connection to the Universe and maintain it in a high state of working order.

Don't give up but believe that everything is possible with love.

Have you sought out like minded people and enjoyed their company?

It can be easy to go on a downwards spiral when things seem to go wrong. However, allocating time to activities like reading inspirational works or listening to soothing music can dispel such feelings. This will help clear your mind, enabling you to establish better contact with your Higher Self.

Have you ever asked for help from the Higher Levels and given up doing your best believing assistance was never coming?
After asking for guidance know that this may take time and come in unusual ways, so keep positive and continue to play your part.

Epilogue:

Change your focus: Raise your Consciousness

Everything you experience is based upon your perception. Any change in your perception alters what you experience. An open mind means always being available to new possibilities, indeed to making changes to your perception. You can assist the Soul by observing and understanding the interaction of cause and effect on these experiences.

If you have a closed mind then you will be unable to alter your perception and this will prevent you from seeing the message or learning the lesson. You will continue to act and behave as you have done up to this point. If you think that you know it all, or think you understand what you know then you have closed your mind to further possibilities. Your enquiring nature stops functioning because your mind does not see any sense in examining what it thinks it knows. When you acknowledge that you do not know or understand something, you are asking your mind to observe, investigate and provide further information.

We believe it is important to set aside some time every day, say about twenty minutes, to allow the mind to quieten down. Thoughts will calm down if you give them the time and opportunity. It also helps to plan your quiet time so that you are able to do it at approximately the same time and in the same place every day. Obviously, the best time is when you can be alone and nothing will disturb you.

In your quiet time, you can ask questions of the Universe. Keep your questions "open" and not "closed". Use "what" and "why" questions to help you understand. What you get back from this type of question helps you to put another that assists you in gaining a deeper and fuller understanding.

Remember, everything is constantly changing. As we have attempted to show you in the body of this book, the moment is always passing and it is important to live in it. Holding on to the past keeps you in the past and prevents you from experiencing something new. The past is the known and cannot be changed. If you learn the lesson or accept the message from it, you will change your focus and this will allow you to let go of the event: you set yourself free to experience something new. Open-ended questions help you do this and complete the detachment process.

Never be tempted to do things in a rush, for you will miss out on what it is you are actually trying to achieve. The slower you move, the less blurred your vision and the more you see. Quiet and attentive observation allows you to see even more. Such a view is free of all distractions, especially thought. All your senses and every part of your being are focused on what you are seeing.

Everything serves a purpose or it ceases to exist. Nothing in life is ever really wasted. Everything you encounter or do in life helps you to grow and evolve. You unknowingly judge life, others and yourself when you allow thought to label something good or bad, right or wrong. Looking at everything as a possibility, a probability or potential resource alters your focus. In turn, you cease to judge and begin to discover opportunities you never knew existed.

You learn what is right by experiencing what is wrong. You live in a world in which there are imperfections so that you can understand perfection. Nothing new would ever be learned if you never erred. Your errors provide the resources needed to learn. When you understand that errors actually help you grow you will be willing to learn the lesson from them. In turn, you learn more and discover how enjoyable learning can be. Life becomes an exciting adventure rather than dull and tedious. Errors are really opportunities.

The Universe ensures that you are always experiencing what you need to experience at the right time. Problems and undesirable predicaments cause you to focus on what you perceive that you do not have. Focusing your attention on what you have alters your perception. Seeing life as your ally rather than your foe allows you to achieve the impossible.

What occurred is not important; what is important is how you respond. It does not matter what happened to you or who did it to you. What matters is what you do about it. You examine the situation, see the message, resolve the problem and prevent it from occurring again.

You learn from observing and embracing differences. Disrupting your routine and embracing differences alters your focus. In turn, you stimulate your growth and diminish your fears. The less fearful you are, the more security you find in the unknown: you will learn to trust the Universe.

Everyone is doing the best they can. It is easy to criticise or judge another, especially yourself. Your expectations of others and yourself prevent you from seeing that everyone is doing the best they can. Unless you can communicate with another's Soul, you have no idea what their Soul desires to experience. Allowing others to be themselves and experience their uniqueness changes your perception. You cease to be critical and begin to value and respect uniqueness. In turn, you become a supportive ally rather than a critical spectator.

Remember you are not alone. In the depths of your depression, despair or anger it is difficult to see that others have experienced what you are experiencing, for life presents difficulties to everyone so that they may learn and grow. Always, there will be someone there to offer the support and comfort you need. Your Higher Self is always available, as are the Angels and other Beings of Light. When you acknowledge and accept that you will find that you are able to grow in confidence and in spirit.

We wish you well on your Spiritual journey.

A

abundance · 32, 46, 49, 82
acceptance · 13
afraid · 13, 20, 79, 80
anger · 15, 28, 44, 49, 52, 58, 67, 70, 79, 86, 95
angry · 30, 66, 70
attitude · 6, 15, 45, 68, 69
awareness · 38, 98

B

balance · 30, 62, 77
beauty · 13, 38, 49, 68, 105
blame · 49, 79

C

change · 5, 13, 14, 15, 18, 28, 30, 38, 44, 45, 55, 56, 59, 66, 71, 73, 77, 79, 80, 82, 92, 95, 96, 98, 102, 107, 110, 118, 124, 128, 132, 135, 136
choice · 57, 92, 99

D

despair · 66, 137

E

Ego · 20, 21, 46, 47, 65, 67, 69, 72, 75, 104, 105
energy · 6, 20, 22, 26, 30, 36, 57, 58, 59, 66, 76, 89, 90, 95, 101, 108, 110, 115
experiences · 34, 49, 52, 72, 84, 92, 109, 112, 135

F

faith · 79

fear · 5, 10, 20, 21, 28, 32, 41, 49, 52, 64, 72, 82
focus · 34, 49, 95, 102
forgiveness · 24, 26, 28, 102, 128
free will · 34, 35, 69, 80, 99
freedom · 11, 47

G

growth · 5, 13, 14, 15, 20, 49, 57, 59, 60
guidance · 22, 60, 75, 79, 84, 85, 92

H

healing · 18, 34, 35, 75, 84, 85, 86, 101
Higher Self · 11, 22, 25, 30, 41, 42, 50, 58, 62, 64, 67, 71, 72, 79, 81, 84, 96
hope · 14, 34, 64, 72, 76
hurt · 24, 25, 30, 32, 67, 75, 79

I

Inner Being · 19, 21, 42, 50, 58, 59, 63, 67, 80
Inner Self · 11, 19, 41, 47, 53, 61, 68, 88, 98, 99, 101, 107, 110, 121
inspiration · 64

J

judgment · 6, 11, 28, 71, 86, 87, 104

M

meditation · 67, 77

P

peace · 6, 26, 44, 52, 81, 82, 89, 101
potential · 5, 13, 14, 29, 57, 92
progress · 10, 12, 13, 15, 28, 42, 55, 57, 72, 79, 86, 104

Living the Spiritual Laws for Health and Abundance

Andrew Hain and Helen W A Hain
ISBN 0-9545446-0-9 (978-0-9545446-0-7) RRP £9.99

Living the Spiritual Laws for Health and Abundance gives a easy-to-follow introduction to 36 Spiritual Laws. Each of the two authors has channelled a short explanation of each Law, thus giving a slightly different angle to the interpretation. You are encouraged to meditate and write your own interpretations.

Living the Spiritual Laws is also a self help guide to living the Laws on a day to day basis. Through questions and meditations you will be helped to identify where each Law fits in relation to everyday living.

In Living the Spiritual Laws you will be guided to
* incorporate the Laws into your life
* keep a daily journal to record events, your reactions and how you could have responded in a more spiritual way
* construct and use affirmations
* follow the 16 steps to Living the Laws

Living the Spiritual Laws will change your approach to life, empowering you to take control and grow spiritually.
Andrew and Helen are experienced Therapists, Healers and Teachers. They have written and presented their workshops extensively.

During a difficult period in their life they turned to channelling on the Spiritual Laws for help and guidance. The answers they received were put into practice, enabling them to let go of fear and use the situations to grow spiritually. They believe that what they have been given is for sharing with others: service is the pathway to Spiritual Enlightenment.

Words of Wisdom for Everyday Living

Andrew Hain and Helen W A Hain

ISBN 0-9545446-1-7 (978-0-9545446-1-4) RRP £7.99

Words of Wisdom for Everyday Living comprises 50 mottoes, each followed by a few paragraphs of explanation channelled by each of the authors. Readers are encouraged to go within themselves to consider how these mottoes can be applied to their everyday lives.

Whilst *Words of Wisdom* can be read through from beginning to end, the authors hope that it will also provide an inspiration in times of difficulty when problems can be helped with a spiritual answer by

- ❖ Taking a few moments quiet to ask for guidance from the Higher Self;
- ❖ Opening the book at random and consider what is being said in that particular motto;
- ❖ Taking on only that which seems appropriate in the motto;
- ❖ Considering the questions at the end of the motto which prompt the reader to apply the information in a way that is right for them.

Words of Wisdom will help you to realise that dealing with life's problems at a Spiritual level is the only way to let go of fear and change your approach to life, empowering you to take control and appreciating that what happens in life does so for a reason.

Words of Wisdom is intended to inspire and guide the reader to seek out answers at a Spiritual level when trying to solve a problem at a physical level has produced no satisfactory answer.

Words of Wisdom is a companion in times of need when a spiritual answer may provide the way forward.

Also from Well Within Therapies

CD: **"Winds of Change"**, three visualisations for Spiritual Development. Running Time 53 minutes.

Card Set : **"Living the Spiritual Laws for Health and Abundance"** Boxed set of 36 cards, each containing a summary of the Spiritual Laws featured in the book of the same name.

Card Set : **"Words of Wisdom for Everyday Living"** Boxed set of 50 cards, each containing one of the mottoes featured in the book of the same name.

Card Set : **"More Words of Wisdom for Everyday Living"** Boxed set of 50 cards, each containing one of the mottoes featured in the book of the same name.

All of the above are available from
Well Within Therapies, 26 Orchard Road, Kingston upon Thames, Surrey, KT1 2QW.

A Home Study Course based on **"Living the Spiritual Laws for Health and Abundance"** is available either by e-mail or regular post. Please contact Well Within Therapies for details or visit the web site www.wellwithintherapies.co.uk.

One day and Two day workshops based on **"Living the Spiritual Laws for Health and Abundance"** are held regularly at various venues in the UK, please see web site for latest dates / venues.